WILLIAM BLAKE
&
HIS POETRY

BY
ALLARDYCE NICOLL

Published by Left of Brain Books

Copyright © 2021 Left of Brain Books

ISBN 978-1-396-31925-9

First Edition

All rights reserved. No part of this publication may be reproduced, distributed, or transmitted in any form or by any means, including photocopying, recording, or other electronic or mechanical methods, without the prior written permission of the publisher, except in the case of brief quotations embodied in critical reviews and certain other noncommercial uses permitted by copyright law. Left of Brain Books is a division of Left Of Brain Onboarding Pty Ltd.

Table of Contents

GENERAL PREFACE	1
WILLIAM BLAKE & HIS POETRY I	3
II	11
III	23
IV	35
V	59
VI	81
VII	97
BIBLIOGRAPHY	101

GENERAL PREFACE

A GLANCE through the pages of this little book will suffice to disclose the general plan of the series of which it forms a part. Only a few words of explanation, therefore, will be necessary.

The point of departure is the undeniable fact that with the vast majority of young students of literature a living interest in the work of any poet can best be aroused, and an intelligent appreciation of it secured, when it is immediately associated with the character and career of the poet himself. The cases are indeed few and far between in which much fresh light will not be thrown upon a poem by some knowledge of the personality of the writer, while it will often be found that the most direct—perhaps even the only—way to the heart of its meaning lies through a consideration of the circumstances in which it had its birth. The purely æsthetic critic may possibly object that a poem should be regarded simply as a self-contained and detached piece of art, having no personal affiliations or bearings. Of the validity of this as an abstract principle nothing need now be said. The fact remains that, in the earlier stages of study at any rate, poetry is most valued and loved when it is made to seem most human and vital; and the human and vital interest of poetry can be most surely brought home to the reader by the biographical method of interpretation.

This is to some extent recognized by writers of histories and text-books of literature, and by editors of selections from the works of our poets; for place is always given by them to a certain amount of biographical material. But in the histories and text-books the biography of a given writer stands by itself, and his work has to be sought elsewhere, the student being left to make the connexion for himself; while even in our current editions of selections there is little systematic attempt to link biography, step by step, with production.

This brings us at once to the chief purpose of the present series. In this, biography and production will be considered together and in intimate, association. In other words, an endeavour will be made to interest the reader in the lives and personalities of the poets dealt with, and at the same time to use biography as an introduction and key to their writings.

Each volume will therefore contain the life story of the poet who forms its subject. In this, attention will be specially directed to his personality as it expressed itself in his poetry, and to the influences and conditions which counted most as formative factors in the growth of his genius. This biographical study will be used as a setting for a selection, as large as space will permit, of his representative poems. Such poems, where possible, will be reproduced in full, and care will be taken bring out their connexion with his character, his circumstances, and the movement of his mind. Then, in addition, so much more general literary criticism will be incorporated as may see to be needed to supplement the biographical material, and to exhibit both the essential qualities and the historical importance of his work.

It is believed that the plan thus pursued is substantially in the nature of a new departure, and that the volumes in this series, constituting as they will an introduction to the study of some of our greatest poets, will be found useful to teachers and students of literature, and no less to the general lover of English poetry.

WILLIAM HENRY HUDSON

WILLIAM BLAKE & HIS POETRY

I

MR CHESTERTON has said that if one wished to pen aright a narrative of the life of William Blake one would have to start with chaos and the creation of the world. If somewhat exaggerated and bizarre, this epigram, like most epigrams, contains a great deal of elemental truth in it, for it seems to emphasize a point that only too often is overlooked– Blake's close and intimate relations with the world around him, his reflection of the past and his vision of the future. All poets, in some way or another, are symbols of their age, but there are some who stand in much closer relations with their surroundings than others. There are poets who maintain a distant aloofness: there are poets who react rather than reflect: there are others, and of these Blake is one of the most noticeable, who catch up new strains of emotion, new thoughts, new ideas, and express them for all time in imperishable language. Not uncommonly, also, we find the last category of poets the peculiar paradox that they, who most reflect and prophesy, are of the greatest individuality, of the most arresting personality. In Italy Petrarca was one of these, a man stamping his imagery on three centuries of poetic endeavour, anticipating the new spirit of humanism to the extent of poring over a Greek volume whose characters even he could barely understand. In England Milton was another, a very mirror of his age, and yet with a character and indomitability of temper hard to equal elsewhere.

This fact is important, for the obstinacy and lack of flexibility in the character of William Blake have led many to regard him as a stray voice crying in the wilderness, unrelated to time or to place. His life was a comparatively lonely one, although perhaps not quite so lonely as many biographers have made out. He was, at any rate, member of no clique or school. Living on to 1827 and the advent of Shelley, Keats, and Byron, he had no personal intercourse with the Lake poets, or Scott, or Lamb, or many of the numerous men of letters with whom the last years of the eighteenth century and the early years of the nineteenth seemed stocked. We are apt to picture him in his garret,

> Singing hymns unbidden,
> Till the world is wrought
> To sympathy with hopes and fears it heeded not.

In Professor Herford's magnificent study of the age of Wordsworth, Blake is barely mentioned a couple of times, and, although Professor Herford does connect him with the "Renascence of Wonder," we feel that lie, like most critics, regards Blake as outside his age, as an individual singer of undoubted beauty, but of small interest when the trends and the tendencies of his age are to be considered.

It is true that Blake had but small influence on writers contemporary with him. His true worth has not been recognized until toward the end of the nineteenth century. His real influence cannot be said to have begun before the enthusiastic admiration of Swinburne and of Rossetti. It has not yet reached its culmination. His associations with the cultured society of his time, however, are not to be neglected, for they are deeper and broader than is generally recognized, although mostly confined to the world of art, and not of poetry. Samuel Palmer, whose testimony we may trust, declared that he never looked "on him as an unfortunate man of genius. He knew every great man of his day and had enough." By 'great men' Palmer meant painters. In 1825 the Royal Academy made him a gift of twenty-five pounds in recognition of the beauty of his designs for Blair's "Grave." He was offered the post of art master to the royal children, an offer he rejected in order to keep his freedom. The "Literary Gazette" of 1827, in noticing his death, declared that "few persons of taste" were unacquainted with his designs. Several of the finest artists of his time were unstinted in their praise both of his imagination and of his technique.

We know too that Wordsworth was introduced to Blake's writings by Crabb Robinson, and is reported to have stated his belief in Blake's madness. "Yet," he added, "yet there is something in the madness of this man which interests me more than the sanity of Lord Byron and Walter Scott." The young German painter Götzenberger announced that he had seen in England many men of talent, but only three men of genius—Coleridge, Flaxman, and Blake—and of these three Blake was the greatest. Lamb was "delighted with the catalogue" of Blake's paintings at Carnaby Street, especially with the critical examination of the Canterbury Pilgrims. Hazlitt "saw no merit" in the designs to Young's "Night Thoughts," but admired intensely several of the poems, while Wainewright, of whom Oscar Wilde has written in his "Pen, Pencil, and Poison," was one of the few men of his own or of any other day brave enough to praise openly the "Jerusalem" and urge it on the public. For him Blake executed what is probably the finest copy in existence of the "Songs of Innocence and of Experience."

Such were Blake's actual relations with the *littérateurs* and the artists of his day, noticeable enough when we consider his uncompromising treatment of would-be superiors. Yet on this rests not a whit of his title to be considered, not only as a precursor, but as a perfect symbol of the Romantic Revival in England. However much he may seem isolated from the Lake poets, or from the neo-Grecian society of Byron, Shelley, and Keats, however much he may seem buried in his Bognor cottage or in his petty London lodgings, Blake shared intensely in the *milieu* of the age. Blake, isolated as he may have been when we compare him with other poets, is a perfect type of the Romantic Revival in its literary, social, and artistic developments.

Two things periods of revolt adduce–individuality and what we may call philosophic anarchism. It was those two forces that spread the greater glories of the Renascence: it was the same forces that inspired the revival. Men reached a new conception of their own value as reasoning beings. They realized their own worth, and the worth of their own emotions as apart from all external rules and commandments. They sought new means of expression, and, recreating, they shattered the old. They searched for, and found, fresh anti-rule tendencies in literature and in life. They demanded liberty and the free expression of individuality, and they won them in the swift heat of revolutionary ardour.

As we shall see when we come to trace the actual facts of his life and the development of his inner consciousness, Blake was of this individualism and antinomianism an extreme exponent and example.

Besides the revival of individualistic thought which characterized the Romantic Revival as it characterized the Renascence, there arose toward the close of the eighteenth century a movement analogous with it, but of a more religious character. This new type of religious enthusiasm was marked by a peculiar mysticism which found expression in forms as diverse as Wordsworth's pantheism, the ritualism of the Oxford Movement, and, later, the Neoplatonism of a man like Maurice Maeterlinck. It swept the deistic attitude of Pope and of his *confrères* into a limbo of neglect. It sought deeper and purer truths of the universe. It allied itself more with literary and philosophic thought—becoming creative and inspired as in ages of Grecian gods and of the Northern sagas of divine adventure. In this new development of religion Blake must assume a capital position. He is linked with Shelley in many of his ideas. He expresses mystical truths the exact counterpart of Wordsworth's more inspired pronouncements. With Blake the myth-weaving power was revived again, so that his poems become peopled with a number of figures as fully delineated and as clear-cut in form and idea as ever were Aphrodite and Zeus.

This new religious idealism looked out upon the world with changed vision. Every one of the Romantic poets saw nature in a fresh light—a light never revealed to the ancients, save in rare magic instants, and barely divined by the poets of the Cinquecento in Italy or of the Elizabethan age in England. This new vision of nature took the form at once of wider divination and of characteristic embodiment of natural presences. In this Wordsworth, Shelley, and Blake stand side by manifesting different conceptions indeed, all three revealing a new spirit in nature, profound and mystical, filled with glorious triumphs of the poetic imagination.

The first fact to be grasped in our study of Blake, and incidentally in any study of Wordsworth and of Shelley, is that he, like them, is absolutely sincere in his faith in the imagination, and more, in what was presented before him through the medium of his imagination. When Wordsworth assures us that

> One impulse from a vernal wood
> May teach you more of man,
> Of moral evil and of good,
> Than all the sages can,

he is not, as some have thought, straining his ideas to an unwarrantable extent, or exaggerating because he saw what evil the "meddling intellect" had created in the past century: he is expressing an emotional faith as deep, as sincere, as any of the utterances of the most convinced of religious preachers. In exactly the same way Blake's visionary forms, created either from his own imagination, or seen through the external forms of nature, were more real to him than the men and women he met in daily life. His vision was "twofold always," as he says in a letter to Thomas Butts dated 1802; sometimes it became fourfold:

> May God us keep
> From single vision, and Newton's sleep!

By "single vision, and Newton's sleep" Blake meant the pure unimaginative use of the intellect, where a primrose is nothing but a primrose, or, worse still, but a botanical specimen for scientific analysis. By double vision he meant that quality of seeing past and through the outward manifestations of nature into the soul that lies within:

> To see a World in a grain of sand,
> And a Heaven in a wild flower,
> Hold Infinity in the palm of your hand,
> And Eternity in an hour.[1]

Under the double vision everything took on for him human semblance:

> Each grain of sand,
> Every stone on the land,
> Each rock and each hill,
> Each fountain and rill,
> Each herb and each tree,
> Mountain, hill, earth, and sea. ...
> Are men seen afar. ...[2]

> For double the vision my eyes do see,
> And a double vision is always with me.

---

[1] "Auguries of Innocence" (from the Pickering MS.).
[2] Letter to Thomas Butts, October 2, 1800.

> With my inward eye, 'tis an Old Man grey,
> With my outward, a Thistle across my way.[3]

"'What?' it will be questioned," he writes in his note on his picture "The Last Judgment." "'When the sun rises do you not see a round disk of fire something like a guinea?' Oh! no! no! I see an innumerable company of the heavenly host crying—'Holy, holy, holy, is the Lord God Almighty!'"

With Wordsworth and Shelley, then, Blake stands as an upholder, as the chief upholder, of the power of the creative imagination. This belief of his led him, like Wordsworth, away from the paths of reason, and caused him to write poems which might appear to more ordinary and mundane people as exaggerated, if not insane. Of the three poets Blake is the most extreme. Shelley never gave himself to such a mystic world as the poet of "Jerusalem" created for himself: Wordsworth always retained contact with the kindred points of heaven and home: Blake alone swept clearly away to a world of his own devising. It is this that partly explains the difficulty—although that difficulty is often exaggerated—of Blake's 'prophetic' poems. The full depth of meaning in "Tintern Abbey" may not be appreciated in an ordinary reading, but it will be more appreciated than even such a simple work as "Thel." It is thus that Blake, by the very fact that he expresses more completely than Wordsworth the ideas and faith which were common to nearly all the Romantic writers, by the fact that he at an earlier date and much more enthusiastically expresses the new atmosphere of his age, has cut himself off from a great deal of the appreciative attention which would otherwise have been his.

Finally, as fully representative of the English Revival, Blake stands forth to us in his literary medium, a medium as characteristic as was that of Keats. Blake was undoubtedly one of the first of our eighteenth-century poets to become conscious of the beauties of our sixteenth- and seventeenth-century verse, and all through his life his denunciation of pseudo-classical precepts and examples was unremitting and severe. In his first volume we find him admirous of precisely all those things which were rising to the surface in the transitional years about 1770 and 1780. These we shall indicate in more detail hereafter, and if these are the only very direct reminiscences of earlier poets in his work, they prove conclusively at least what it was that fed his youthful

---

[3] Letter to Thomas Butts, November 22, 1802.

talents, what laid the foundation of his art. Later we find him illustrating Young's "Night Thoughts" and Blair's "Grave," two of the gloomy poems which make up part of a transitional school midway between the urbanity of Pope and the romantic strangeness of the later writers. We find him illustrating Dante, last flower of medieval life. We find all through his work the prevailing influence of "Ossian" and of the revival of Celtic mythology and ideas. From first to last Blake was dominated by his admiration of Gothic art. One of his earliest biographers and friends declared that he had almost become a "Gothic monument" himself, and this, in consideration of Blake's own pronouncements and of his own art, is a term entirely felicitous. Almost the first objects—save nature itself—which moulded his fancy were the antique tombs of Westminster Abbey, which, day after day, he was sent to copy by his master, Basire, the engraver. These tombs impressed themselves on his mind, and probably were the inspiring force for his "King Edward the Third." Within the vast and fretted cathedral, perched on a scaffolding high among its wonders, he must have felt the spirit of the Middle Ages penetrating within him, so that all that was cold and precise and hard he came to despise as 'Grecian,' thus cutting himself off from one branch of romantic inspiration—that which led Shelley and Keats and Byron to a study of the life and literature of Athens. The gods of Greece and of Egypt, he declared in an incensed moment, "were Mathematical Diagrams," forgetting, or not knowing of, the beautiful images of Osiris, the profound tale of Prometheus, or the delicate imagery of Eros and Psyche. "Gothic," he announced again, "is Living Form," and that, for him, was "Eternal Existence." In that pronouncement is the most precise and succinct critical declaration of his principle in art. His visions were living, not cold mathematical things.

The ages of revolt are always "Gothic" in their neglect of rule and of formulated precision, "Gothic" in their insistence on the inherent unity and loveliness of each separate art product as distinct from extraneous rules or fixed methods of judgment. Blake's insistence on Gothic as meaning antinomian, individualistic creation and contempt of rule only symbolizes the movement of which he forms a part, and the fact that he does so becomes all the more interesting and important when we consider that he rose to manhood untutored and had to form his taste for himself. Although he was born in a time when a new movement was on foot, there was nothing to guide him in the way he adopted. That way he chose naturally and unconsciously. His literary preferences were made as if by instinct, for in his younger days the pseudo-classic ideal was paramount. When, in his boyhood, he attended sales at Christie's and at Langford's, and bought there prints which no one was as yet asking for, but which now are regarded as priceless, both monetarily and artistically, we feel that the aura of a spiritual temper had settled upon him as a halo on a saint. Langford, as Malkin tells us, called Blake his "little connoisseur," but to explain that quality in him which made him pass by Reynolds and Lawrence and all the Academicians, which made him despise Pope and Johnson, which urged him to a love of Elizabethan poems and of Gothic architecture, involves a problem whose solution is beyond us, because unexplored and untried. It is our duty alone to note the facts, and leave the reasoning to a future age. In any case, was it not fitting that this man, whose whole being was cast into a series of symbols, should himself be the pre-eminent symbol of his age?

II

LIKE so many others of our poets and prose-writers, Blake is to be connected, if but hazily and remotely, with the Celtic races. His father was a London hosier, with a shop at 28 Broad Street, Golden Square, one James Blake by name, apparently a scion of the famous Irish family of the O'Neils, and just possibly the illegitimate son of the political revolutionary John O'Neil. From what we know of the poet's later mysticism and of his rebellious tendencies, there is nothing in his character to belie this supposition. William Blake, born on November 28, 1757, was the second of five children, the eldest of whom became a successful merchant and in later life grew estranged, as was but natural, from his genius brother. Of the others, John, who enlisted in the army and died at an early age, appears to have turned out badly and developed in Blake's later visions into "the Evil One," while Robert was the one most akin to the poet in temper and in spirit, appearing symbolically in the "Prophetic Books." Of Catherine, the only daughter, we know very little.

Not many facts have been preserved to us of Blake's early life, but what we do know well reveals to us the man who was to be. Never was there a more pronounced illustration of the truth of Wordsworth's dictum that the child is father of the man. At the age of four, we are told by Crabb Robinson, the boy declared that he saw God put His forehead in at the window, and when he was seven, at Peckham Rye, a tree full of angels appeared before his wondering sight. For these visions he was beaten by his Nonconformist father, as he was by his mother, so Tatham tells us, for running in and saying he had seen "the prophet Ezekiel under a tree in the fields." Blake probably never forgot those chastisements. The visions of his childhood were so real to him, as real as were the visions of his later years, and his hatred of Oppression was so great, that it would indeed have been a wonder if he *had* forgiven. It was probably due to this that he discovered very early in his life that he had in him a spiritual force which owed no allegiance to the dictates of any father or of any mother.

> No earthly parents I confess:
> I am doing my Father's business,

he makes Christ exclaim in "The Everlasting Gospel," and we can read behind the lines to see that he was thinking too of his own case. His mother died in 1792, and the record of the son's emotions is contained in that poem "To Tirzah" in the "Songs of Experience":

TO TIRZAH

> Whate'er is born of mortal birth
> Must be consumed with the earth,
> To rise from generation free:
> Then what have I to do with thee?
>
> The sexes sprung from shame and pride,
> Blow'd in the morn: in evening died;
> But Mercy chang'd death into sleep;
> The sexes rose to work and weep.
>
> Thou, Mother of my mortal part,
> With cruelty didst mould my heart,
> And with false self-deceiving tears
> Didst bind my nostrils, eyes, and ears;
>
> Didst close my tongue in senseless clay,
> And me to mortal life betray:
> The death of Jesus set me free:
> Then what have I to do with thee?

There is much of Blake's later symbolism in this poem, but we can see clearly enough what the poet would say. You merely, he would declare, brought me to life in this world: it was heaven that gave me visions, and even those you strove to restrain. From the time that he grew to manhood William Blake drifted away from his parental home.

In his childhood and boyhood, too, Blake's eager use of pen and of pencil seemed to denote that he was destined for the pictorial arts, and indeed to the end of his life his income was largely derived from his engraving. He was trained to be a painter, not a man of letters: and we must always remember in dealing with his art that he is to be regarded as a new and dominant force as much in design as in poetry. His first master was a certain Mr Pars, who had a drawing school in the Strand. With him he studied for a year or two, and then, at the age of fourteen, in 1771, he was apprenticed to Basire, the engraver, of Great Queen Street, Lincoln's Inn Fields. During all this time Blake was labouring at perfecting his technical ability both in drawing and engraving, and, as we know from his poems, his leisure hours must have been devoted to devouring all the books which he could come across. The literary reminiscences in his first poems prove conclusively that he must have been an omnivorous and yet tasteful reader, a fact that becomes all the more surprising when we consider that he had no one to guide him and that he was daily toiling at another art. He must have spent much time over Milton: he must have studied Shakespeare carefully: he must have read many plays and lyrics of the other Elizabethan and Jacobean stars, from Jonson and Fletcher to Webster and Tourneur. He read, that is to say, all those works which were to play such an enormous part in forming the minds and tempers of the transitional and Romantic poets. Nor did his preferences differ when he came to more modern works. He left Dr Johnson, then the unchallenged dictator of letters, severely alone, and turned eagerly to the heralds of the newer age, as yet unborn. He read Chatterton's Rowley poems (issued 1770), Percy's "Reliques" (1765), and, above all others, Macpherson's "Ossian." In Chatterton he got the pseudo-Gothic atmosphere and the exquisite verbal melodies borrowed largely from Milton's early poems and from the Elizabethans: in Percy he got the free emotional expression of folk-sorrows and folk-joys: in "Ossian" he got the spirit of the Celt, a new prose-music, and a vastness of atmosphere unknown to Johnson and his clique. "Ossian" is now derided. It has been proved a forgery, but we must beware against letting our knowledge of its modern and spurious origin influence our critical appreciation of its merits. Had "Ossian" been merely a forgery, and nothing more, it would not have gripped such minds as those of Cesarotti in Italy, Goethe in Germany, Blake and others in England. It would not have penetrated into the most distant of lands, and served, as in Poland, to awake romantic feelings for a long time dead. While we recognize that Hazlitt is overstating the case when he places

"Ossian" alongside of Homer and of Dante, we must admit that, if it cannot take the highest, it may take an intermediate place. "Ossian" has romance: in places it has grandeur: if it is monotonous, it has in its initial conception just such a sublimity as a young poet of Blake's calibre required. "Ossian" first, then, with Milton, Shakespeare, the Elizabethans, Chatterton, and Percy, were the main literary forces that were moulding the childhood of William Blake. Already, as we have seen, in the sister art he had discovered the Gothic gloom of Westminster Abbey, the mighty force of Michelangelo, the perfect precision of Raphael. On the one side he ignored Pope and Johnson, on the other Rubens and Bartolozzi.

A poet or a painter, however, is not created by and fed on literary or artistic models alone. The temperament of a genius is always full of emotion, often precocious emotion, and in Blake's early tramps into the country—he was ever an indefatigable walker—he came upon two things, nature and love. Born in London as he was, Blake was always a passionate lover of the country, and early and late his poems make constant appeal for a new conception of leaf and flower and bird.

AUGURIES OF INNOCENCE

A robin redbreast in a cage
Puts all Heaven in a rage.
A dove-house fill'd with doves and pigeons
Shudders Hell thro' all its regions.
A dog starv'd at his master's gate
Predicts the ruin of the State.

. . . .

A horse misus'd upon the road
Calls to Heaven for human blood.

. . . .

Each outcry of the hunted hare
A fibre from the brain does tear;

> A skylark wounded in the wing,
> A cherubim does cease to sing.
>
> He who shall hurt the little wren
> Shall never be belov'd by men.
>
> . . . .
>
> The wanton boy that kills the fly
> Shall feel the spider's enmity.
>
> . . . .
>
> The caterpillar on the leaf
> Repeats to thee thy mother's grief.
> Kill not the moth nor butterfly,
> For the Last Judgement draweth nigh.

With his tendency to view all things in the light of eternity, also, he was, as one critic says, passionately in love with the eternal feminine, into which any pair of eyes would serve as windows. The particular pair of bright eyes that captivated him belonged to a lively little girl, a flirt apparently, called Polly Wood. We know little of this Polly Wood, but seemingly she cast him off, and the boy, stung to the heart by this faithlessness and flippancy, fell into despondency. Possibly because of his despair, he grew ill, and was sent to a market-garden at Richmond to recuperate. There he met the market-gardener's daughter, one Catherine Boucher, an uneducated, sympathetic girl, to whom he told his story. "I pity you from my heart," she cried when he had finished. "Do you pity me?" was the poet's answer. "Then I love you for *that*." William Blake and Catherine Boucher were married on August 18, 1782, and were to remain close comrades—there is no other word for it—till death took the poet away in 1827. After their marriage they settled down at 23 Green Street, Leicester Fields.

By this time Blake had already shown, amply we think to-day, what was in him. About the age of twelve, certainly before he was fourteen, he had written verses the like of which had not been heard in England since Milton died.

SONG

How sweet I roam'd from field to field
And tasted all the summer's pride,
Till I the Prince of Love beheld
Who in the sunny beams did glide!

He show'd me lilies for my hair,
And blushing roses for my brow;
He led me through his gardens fair
Where all his golden pleasures grow.

With sweet May dews my wings were wet,
And Phoebus fir'd my vocal rage;
He caught me in his silken net,
And shut me in his golden cage.

He loves to sit and hear me sing,
Then, laughing, sports and plays with me;
Then stretches out my golden wing,
And mocks my loss of liberty.

Those verses are triply interesting. They show the wonderful precociousness of Blake: they show his tendency to inner thought: they show already his delight in allegory and in mysticism. The use of flowers for symbolic purposes is the same as in the "Songs of Innocence and of Experience"; while the employment of gold as a metal of meaning may be paralleled in many a later passage.

Of the exact date of Blake's other early songs we know nothing, but in all probability every one of the poems contained in the volume called "Poetical Sketches," printed in 1783, was written before 1777, at which date Blake was but twenty. By 1773 he had engraved his plate, "Joseph of Arimathea among the Rocks of Albion," showing that already he had formulated at least part of his symbolic system. By 1780 he had met and made friends with Stothard, Flaxman, and Fuseli, and had exhibited at the Royal Academy. Toward the close of 1782 he had been introduced by Flaxman to one of the chiefs of the so-called 'Blue-stockings,' Mrs Mathew, of 27 Rathbone Place.

This Mrs Mathew was the wife of a clergyman, and was the proud possessor of a *salon* where art and literature were discussed decorously over innumerable cups of tea. She and her husband would seem to have welcomed the young poet-artist and his wife. We hear of Blake Singing his own songs there to an enraptured company, and it was at the expense of Mathew and of Fuseli that the volume of "Poetical Sketches" was printed. Of the exact details of what happened, again we are ignorant. Perhaps Blake in his pride objected generally to being patronized, perhaps Mr Mathew's kindly meant but unfortunately worded preface aroused the artist's ire. "The following sketches," says Mathew, "were the production of untutored youth, commenced in his twelfth and occasionally resumed by the author till his twentieth year. ... *Conscious of the irregularities and defects to be found in almost every page, his friends have still believed that they possessed a poetical originality, which merited some respite from oblivion.*" The italicized phrases (which were of course not so italicized in the original) were exactly of the type to offend deeply the soul of Blake. Blake was ever conscious of his genius, impatient of restraint, contemptuous of that meticulous care and polish that marks the verse of Pope. "Improvement makes straight roads," he wrote later in "The Marriage of Heaven and Hell," "but the crooked roads without improvement are the roads of Genius."

Nowadays we can easily picture the scene–the poet, his pride hurt and angry, the patron, conscious of his beneficence and offended at what he must have regarded as the overweening confidence of his *protégé*. We too can detect the irregularities and defects that irritated Mathew. We can see that Blake has repetitions which a minute's care would have put right. In one song the joys are "singing sweet"–"sweet the boughs perfume the air"–"sweet he hears a mournful song"; in another (the one already quoted) "sweet" he roams from field to field, his wings wet with "sweet May dews"; in another is a "sweet village," repeated in yet another as "that sweet village, where my black-eyed maid doth drop a tear." From these few examples, culled at random and occurring in but three pages of print, we can see a lack of verbal curiosity. What we are enabled to see, however, more clearly than Mr Mathew could see, is that Blake was not one of those men who reach the heights by writing and rewriting, but that when he gained perfect felicity of diction it was from his first original inspiration. In a number of his works he altered words here and there, as is evident if we glance at the *apparatus criticus* of the "Oxford" edition of the poems, but he rarely deviated from the form of his first initial phrasing, quite clearly the result of sudden inspiration.

And of that inspiration, fed from past literary models, this tiny volume is full. The way in which this young poet of under twenty has taken melodies and reminiscences from earlier writers and transfused them 'with his own thought is well-nigh marvellous. The "Spring," Summer," "Autumn" (so redolent of Keats), and "Winter" have been inspired by Spenser, with other echoes from Thomson. Akin to them are "To the Evening Star" and "To Morning," besides the more definite "Imitation of Spenser." "Fair Elenor" and "Gwin, King of Norway" are ballads, now in the style of the 'graveyard' school, now in that of the school of barbaric heroism. There are songs which might have come from plays about the beginning of the seventeenth century. "Blind Man's Buff" is a realistic *genre* subject almost in the style of Burns. There is a fragment of a drama, "King Edward the Third," clearly influenced by Shakespeare, and a series of prose extracts derived from a keen study of "Ossian."

Literary models, however, have little to do with the intrinsic beauty of a poem, and in 'any case this first volume is unique in Blake's work, as being the only one much influenced by preceding poets. It is evidently the apprentice work of the poet, written before he had quite formulated his own individual style and utterance. Yet, from the very first, Blake was an absolute master of his craft. Nothing could perfect or better that magnificent invocation "To the Muses," deemed worthy of inclusion in our "Golden Treasury."

TO THE MUSES

Whether on Ida's shady brow,
Or in the chambers of the East,
The chambers of the sun, that now
From ancient melody have ceas'd;

Whether in Heaven ye wander fair,
Or the green corners of the earth,
Or the blue regions of the air
Where the melodious winds have birth;

Whether on crystal rocks ye rove,
Beneath the bosom of the sea,
Wand'ring in many a coral grove;
Fair Nine, forsaking Poetry!

How have you left the ancient love
That bards of old enjoy'd in you!
The languid strings do scarcely move!
The sound is forc'd, the notes are few!

From this we see Blake's idea of contemporary verse, as from the song "My Silks and Fine Array" we can trace one of the ways by which he would recall it to life again.

SONG

My silks and fine array,
My smiles and languish'd air,
By love are driv'n away;
And mournful lean Despair
Brings me yew to deck my grave;
Such end true lovers have.

His face is fair as heav'n
When springing buds unfold;
O why to him was't giv'n,
Whose heart is wintry cold?
His breast is love's all-worshipp'd tomb,
Where all love's pilgrims come.

Bring me an axe and spade,
Bring me a winding-sheet;
When I my grave have made,
Let winds and tempests beat:
Then down I'll lie, as cold as clay.
True love doth pass away!

Failures there are, as there are failures in the work of all poets, but in this, the first fruits of Blake's genius, there is a little galaxy of poems, written with absolute precision, prefiguring at once the gentler songs of innocence, and their terrible answers of experience. The poetic 'felicity' is here, the result, as we saw, of sudden inspiration. The imagery of that last stanza of "Gwin":

> From tow'r to tow'r the watchmen cry,
> "O, Gwin, the son of Nore,
> Arouse thyself! the nations, black
> As clouds, come rolling o'er!"

could hardly be bettered. Of the "Mad Song," Professor Saintsbury exclaims that "for pure verse effect ... there are few pieces in English or in any other language to beat this marvellous thing." Noticeable in it are the skilful substitution of feet, and the mood, premonitory of Blake's later visionary temper.

MAD SONG

The wild winds weep,
And the night is a-cold;
Come hither, Sleep,
And my griefs unfold:
But lo! the morning peeps
Over the eastern steeps,
And the rustling beds of dawn
The earth do scorn.

Lo! to the vault
Of paved heaven,
With sorrow fraught
My notes are driven:
They strike the ear of night,
Make weep the eyes of day;
They make mad the roaring winds,
And with tempests play.

> Like a fiend in a cloud,
> With howling woe
> After night I do crowd
> And with night will go;
> I turn my back to the east
> From whence comforts have increas'd;
> For light doth seize my brain
> With frantic pain.

Even the weaker and more imitative "Seasons" betray excellency of phrase, and one may realize how far Blake's genius for verse-effect extends, when one places such a comparatively insignificant fragment as that "To the Evening Star" beside Mr Robert Bridges' rendering of it into somewhat artificial alcaics.

> O'er bloom the frowning front of awful
> Night to a glance of unearthly silver,

Mr Bridges writes, rendering thus Blake's exquisite and unforgettable

> Speak silence with thy glimmering eyes,
> And wash the dusk with silver.

The one has poetic inspiration, careless but genuine, the other a studied crystallization of phrase, full of those "vast petrific forms" which Blake himself spent all his lifetime in denouncing. In spite of careless verbal finish, Blake attained, in this as in later poems, to the height of his craft, some of his sentences being hardly less rich, less burdened with autumn fruits, than are those of Keats. In fact, one would sometimes think, reading the "Poetical Sketches," that Keats had, indeed, at some time, come to a perusal of them. This may be a vain fancy and is certainly an improbable one, but the lines "To Autumn" recall the famous "Ode," just as the couplet of the song already quoted,

> He show'd me lilies for my hair,
> And blushing roses for my brow,

summons to our mind a similar pair of lines in "La Belle Dame sans Merci," and just as lines like that "whispering faint murmurs to the scanty breeze" bring to us memories of our most jewelled of Singers.

III

TO treat thus largely of Blake's earliest and in many ways least important volume was necessary for the fact that, whereas in one way it displays in embryo Blake's future characteristics, in another it stands unique among his productions. We see there the philosopher, the lyrist, the mystic of coming years, but we also see, what we cannot observe in his later work to anything like so great an extent, the imitator of our own literary glories. This volume both explains Blake's poetic development and gives us a more illuminating portrait of him in relation to his age than would otherwise have been possible. We know from these "Poetical Sketches" that Blake, any more than Shakespeare or Shelley, was not a pure innovator. The ancient triumphs of English song fed his genius and the rhythm of the "Songs of Innocence," no less than that of "Jerusalem," owes its beauty to early study of bygone, and in his age forgotten, masterpieces.

Meanwhile we must return to the record of Blake's life. In 1784, two years after his marriage, with his brother Robert as pupil and one Parker, a former fellow-apprentice, as partner, he opened a print-seller's shop at 27 Broad Street, a venture which, as might have been expected from one of Blake's calibre, was a complete failure. We know again very little of the details of his life during this time. His brother Robert died in February 1787, Blake himself tending him in his illness and watching his soul, clapping its hands for joy, leave the dead body and fly into the heavens. The same year the partnership with Parker was broken. All this time, and for many years after, Blake must have been reading heavily in Sweden-borgian and other schools of mystical thought, the influence of which is to be seen in almost all of his works save the "Poetical Sketches." A fuller account of the symbolic and philosophical ideas which he evolved for himself out of that study we may leave until later. Much more important for the moment is Blake's discovery of a unique method of printing.

By J. T. Smith we are told that the secret of this process was revealed to Blake in a vision of his dead brother Robert, although in a manuscript of the date of about 1783, "An Island in the Moon," we find that already Blake had been contemplating some such plan. The truth perhaps is that from very early times the poet, who was also an artist, had been meditating some means whereby he might reproduce his own works, by his own exertions, unaided by critical patron or commercial publisher, and that about 1788 the particular invention came to him in a flash of inspiration. We are told that when it did come to him he and his wife had but half a crown in the whole world. One shilling and tenpence of that half-crown went to buy the necessary materials. Then Blake set to work.

In simple words the invention consisted in the writing (in reversed letters) of the poems and in the drawing of the illustrative sketches on a copper plate, the ink used being a kind of varnish impervious to acid. The whole plate was then coated with aqua fortis, and the parts not drawn or written on were corroded away, leaving in relief the words and the illustrations. From these plates prints were then taken, and the drawings hand-coloured by washes of paint. All of Blake's poems, save the "Poetical Sketches" and "The French Revolution," were thus produced.

Obviously this process has both advantages and disadvantages. It allows of an intimate relationship between word and design, the whole forming a perfect and unique piece of combined art. It means that each separate off-print will bear its own mark of individuality. Certainly no two copies of any of Blake's volumes are precisely alike. It relieves the poet from the necessity of seeking painfully and perhaps in vain for a publisher of his wares. On the other hand, it means that the poet is able to alter, transpose, or delete separate pages of his poems as he cares, a danger not very great in the case of one of classical tendencies, but fatal almost for a poet of Blake's impetuosity. It necessitates, too, a very scanty productivity, the volumes being issued rather to order than for general sale. This partly explains Blake's isolated position among his fellow-workers, and also the fact that few of his original volumes are now in existence. Of the "Songs of Innocence and of Experience" there are under thirty copies known: of "Jerusalem" and "Ahania" but one each. Until Blake's poems were printed coldly in type there was no hope that he would grow in fame or in popularity, although we must ever remember that the composite arts of the artist's own volumes bring to us finer emotions than do the poems as they are printed in our own times.

The labour which the production of these volumes entailed is hinted at in a letter dated April 12, 1827, and addressed to George Cumberland. "You are desirous, I know," writes Blake, "to dispose of some of my works, but having none remaining of all I have printed, I cannot print more except at a great loss. I am now painting a set of the 'Songs of Innocence and Experience' for a friend at ten guineas. The last work I produced is a poem entitled 'Jerusalem, the Emanation of the Giant Albion,' but find that to print it will cost my time the amount of twenty guineas. One I have finished, but it is not likely I shall find a customer for it. As you wish me to send you a list with the prices, they are as follows:

	£	s.	d.
'America'	6	6	0
'Europe'	6	6	0
'Visions,' etc.	5	5	0
'Thel'	3	3	0
'Songs of Innocence and Experience'	10	10	0
'Urizen'	6	6	0

The first poetic fruits of this new discovery was the volume called "Songs of Innocence," printed in 1789, which, five years afterward, in 1794, was followed by the "Songs of Experience." Those five years separating the two works were truly five years of 'experience' for Blake, but the two little volumes are so closely bound to one another in plan and in substance that they must be treated together. In the main the various songs contained in these two collections are written in pairs, a song of innocence corresponding to a song of experience, but this does not entirely exhaust the series. To "The Lamb" corresponds "The Tiger"; to the "Infant Joy," "Infant Sorrow"; to the "Nurse's Song" of "Innocence," the "Nurse's Song" of "Experience." Indeed, all the earlier songs of "Innocence" have been, with one or two exceptions, copied, or rather contrasted, in the later poems, with the addition in the "Songs of Experience" of a number of verses for which there is no corresponding prototype in the volume of 1789. The poems of these two small volumes compare as they should with those of the "Poetical Sketches." They exhibit, at one and the same time, identical characteristics of the poetic genius and a gradual and general development in poetic power. Their rhythm is easier, their melodies, their measures, are more subtle than all but the very best in the earlier volume. There is lost all attempt at translation, save in the most general way. The words are not eighteenth century, but neither are they Elizabethan. They are Blake's own, now.

Blake's earlier genius is here seen at its best. "The two contrary States of the Human Soul" suited him—for he was not, as indeed few lyric poets are, a deep psychologist of the soul. Blake dealt in elemental visions, and, deep and profound as are many of his emotions, he rarely searched subtly into the rarer manifestations of the spirit. He was joyous or sad: under the rigid rule of Urizen (law and reason) or the anarchic one of Los (inspiration and freedom): within Vala's veils (the deceits of sense) or in the tender bosom of Jerusalem (the realm of the spirit).[4] Songs of Optimism and songs of Pessimism, they might have been called—songs of Melancholy and songs of Joy—the one breathing forth an innocent happiness, ignorant of the evils of the world and seeing God everywhere, and the second, disillusioned, viewing the created universe, not as Shelley's vast dome of life staining the white radiance of eternity, but as a dark blot shutting off the sunlight from a despairing humanity.

HOLY THURSDAY[5]

'Twas on a Holy Thursday, their innocent faces clean,
The children walking two and two, in red, and blue, and green,
Grey-headed beadles walk'd before, with wands as white as snow,
Till into the high dome of Paul's they like Thames' waters flow.

O what a multitude they seem'd, these flowers of London town!
Seated in companies they sit with radiance all their own.
The hum of multitudes was there, but multitudes of lambs,
Thousands of little boys and girls raising their innocent hands.

Now like a mighty wind they raise to Heaven the voice of song,
Or like harmonious thunderings the seats of Heaven among.

---

[4] For Blake's symbolic figures, see page 43 ff.
[5] From "Songs of Innocence."

Beneath them sit the aged men, wise guardians of the poor;
Then cherish pity, lest you drive an angel from your door.

So Blake sang, let us say, about 1785. In 1794 the same vision, seen with different eyes, called forth only a hymn of reproach and of despair.

HOLY THURSDAY[6]

Is this a holy thing to see
In a rich and fruitful land,
Babes reduc'd to misery,
Fed with cold and usurous hand?

Is that trembling cry a song?
Can it be a song of joy?
And so many children poor?
It is a land of poverty!

And their sun does never shine,
And their fields are bleak and bare,
And their ways are fill'd with thorns:
It is eternal winter there.

For where'er the sun does shine,
And where'er the rain does fall,
Babe can never hunger there,
Nor poverty the mind appal.

Blake can never see intermediate states. His is the mind of the extremist. This contrast is everywhere apparent. We are either listening to idyllic songs of Arcady or trembling through miserable streets, more cold and desolate than London's are. We are never, we might almost feel, entirely in this world, but are withdrawn to regions of the imagination where visual phenomena and ordinary emotions are intensified or changed according as the light varies under which we regard them.

---

[6] From "Songs of Experience."

The "Songs of Innocence" are beautifully prefaced by an "Introduction" with which they open, and which for music and for sentiment is among the finer lyrics of Blake.

INTRODUCTION

Piping down the valleys wild,
Piping songs of pleasant glee,
On a cloud I saw a child,
And he laughing said to me:

"Pipe a song about a Lamb!"
So I piped with merry cheer.
"Piper, pipe that song again!"
So I piped: he wept to hear.

"Drop thy pipe, thy happy pipe;
Sing thy songs of happy cheer:"
So I sang the same again,
While he wept with joy to hear.

"Piper, sit thee down and write
In a book, that all may read."
So he vanish'd from my sight;
And I pluck'd a hollow reed,

And I made a rural pen,
And I stained the water clear,
And I wrote my happy songs
Every child may joy to hear.

It is the child however, youthful of soul and not necessarily youthful of body, who will joy to listen to those songs. For, despite their tender grace and their childlike simplicity, not even the "Songs of Innocence" will charm entirely the heart of extremest youth. That charm, comes only to the youthful and the visionary of soul, who see in these re-creations of a Golden Age, an age of innocence manifestations of the spirit in its purest form. A child may repeat

> Little Lamb, who made thee?
> Dost thou know who made thee!

and gain therefrom childish pleasure: but in reality, the full worth of the poem can be felt only by the aged in wisdom who return to the delicate and simple emotions, subtly enunciated, contained in that poem and in all the other poems of the "Songs of Innocence."

There is this peculiar paradox in these "Songs of Innocence and of Experience," that, though they shadow forth Blake's philosophy of life, their rhythm and wording are the simplest that possibly could be imagined. No heavy-laden or mystic words meet our eyes. The phrases sound as innocent as a child's laughter, yet there is hidden with them a wealth of meaning.

INFANT JOY

> "I have no name;
> I am but two days old."
> What shall I call thee?
> "I happy am,
> Joy is my name."
> Sweet joy befall thee!
>
> Pretty Joy!
> Sweet Joy, but two days old.
> Sweet Joy I call thee:
> Thou dost smile,
> I sing the while;
> Sweet joy befall thee!

There is simplicity in that: but there is profound art. We are sometimes annoyed yet by Blake's insistence on a single word—as "sweet" in this or in "The Shepherd"—but we forgive it now, even more readily than in the "Poetical Sketches," because of the perfect simplicity of youthful happiness, a happiness that is only intensified by the bitter terror of its counterpart in "Experience":

INFANT SORROW

My mother groan'd, my father wept,
Into the dangerous world I leapt,
Helpless, naked, piping loud,
Like a fiend hid in a cloud.

Struggling in my father's hands,
Striving against my swaddling bands,
Bound and weary, I thought best
To sulk upon my mother's breast.

These two atmospheres, the two moods, contrary states of the human soul, are eternal: and it is their conflict that gives beauty and value to the work of Blake, the one tender simplicity of loving thought, the other a bitterness of invective and of condemning pride.

To Mercy, Pity, Peace, and Love
All pray in their distress;
And to these virtues of delight
Return their thankfulness.[7]

he sang in the earlier book, and then, in a fierce fury of hatred and of horror, all these tender qualities seemed to him nothing but evil, hypocritical and serpent-like in their luring power:

Pity would be no more
If we did not make somebody poor:
And Mercy no more could be
If all were as happy as we.[8]

On the one hand is purity, truth, love, and on the other those same qualities of purity, truth, and love transformed into agents directly negative and directly antagonistic to themselves—charity a thing born of misery, pity of oppression.

---

[7] "The Divine Image."
[8] "The Human Abstract."

By understanding something of this philosophy which was forming in the soul of Blake, we are enabled to see more clearly the symbolic force of those two most popular poems in the two collections, "The Lamb" and "The Tiger." They, indeed, might be taken as mottoes respectively of the two books. Like most of Blake's early poems, their finished artistry of phrasing allows them to be read with delight even if we do not care to stop and consider their expression of Blake's philosophy; but for a true realization of their force they must be closely connected with the other poems that go along with them as well as with the peculiar system of philosophy and of symbolic forces which, as we shall see, Blake at this very time was evolving for himself out of his reading of the mystics.

THE LAMB

Little Lamb, who made thee?
Dost thou know who made thee?
Gave thee life, and bid thee feed,
By the stream and o'er the mead;
Gave thee clothing of delight,
Softest clothing, woolly, bright;
Gave thee such a tender voice,
Making all the vales rejoice?
　Little Lamb, who made thee?
　Dost thou know who made thee?
　Little Lamb, I'll tell thee;
　Little Lamb, I'll tell thee:
He is callèd by thy name,
For He calls Himself a Lamb.
He is meek, and He is mild;
He became a little child.
I a child, and thou a lamb,
We are callèd by his name.
　Little Lamb, God bless thee!
　Little Lamb, God bless thee!

THE TIGER

Tiger! Tiger! burning bright
In the forests of the night,
What immortal hand or eye
Could frame thy fearful symmetry?

In what distant deeps or skies
Burnt the fire of thine eyes?
On what wings dare he aspire?
What the hand dare seize the fire?

And what shoulder, and what art,
Could twist the sinews of thy heart?
And when thy heart began to beat,
What dread hand? and what dread feet?

What the hammer? what the chain?
In what furnace was thy brain?
What the anvil? what dread grasp
Dare its deadly terrors clasp?

When the stars threw down their spears,
And water'd heaven with their tears,
Did he smile his work to see?
Did he who made the Lamb make thee?

Tiger! Tiger! burning bright
In the forests of the night,
What immortal hand or eye
Dare frame thy fearful symmetry?

Such is the intellectual and emotional content of these books, revealing in lyric verse what were to be the two great conflicting ideas in Blake's later development, although those ideas are but hazily sketched out at this stage in his career. Mr Ellis calculated that Blake formed his symbolic system between the years 1788 and 1790, just the very years that lie between "Innocence" and

"Experience." Nor does this first era of definite symbolism harm the poetic content of even the later songs. "If," says Swinburne, "if the 'Songs of Innocence' have the shape and smell of leaves and of buds, these [the "Songs of Experience"] have in them the light and sound of fire or the sea"—a sentence which, when we consider it closely, seems profound with meaning. In the "Introduction" to "Experience" and in "Earth's Answer" we are first met with ideas we cannot fathom unless we have the key wherewith to unlock the flood-gate of these peerless waters: yet, having that key, our joy and our admiration must be increased an hundredfold. In the "Poetical Sketches" we have splendid lyrics: lyrics, however, not distinctively Blake's own in the matter of form or words. In "Innocence" we have his first free expression of life, hardly troubled with philosophy, save in a few sentences, in a few ideas half hidden in childlike thought. In "Experience" his knowledge and his wisdom have expanded to give a full fruit of poetry, bearing exquisite form, fresh fervor, and symbolic content, all magically wrought together. It is this union of thought and of emotion of form and of content, that gives us the great masterpieces of art.

In "Experience", too, we come upon a maturer artist. In "Innocence," as we saw, the poet lisped, talked simply to the humble and the childlike of heart. Here he speaks more deliberately to those old in wisdom, who have felt life's bitterness and yearn, as an exile yearns, for an antique home of rest. Before we pass from these two well-known little volumes, let me quote just one more poem from the "Songs of Experience."

AH! SUN-FLOWER

> Ah, Sun-flower! weary of time,
> Who countest the steps of the sun;
> Seeking after that sweet golden clime,
> Where the traveller's journey is done;
>
> Where the Youth pined away with desire,
> And the pale Virgin shrouded in snow,
> Arise from their graves, and aspire
> Where my Sun-flower wishes to go.

I do not intend at present to enter into the full symbolism of that poem, but we may note that of symbolism it is full. It is to be linked closely with Blake's other more general ideas concerning inspiration, his heaven of free spirits and his hatred of the world. For him birth in this earth came to mean a lying in the grave, where all the finest impulses of the spirit were checked and restrained. In this poem he takes the sunflower as the symbol of a soul aspiring to reach the sun, the sun that is so like it and yet is so far away. It turns toward the sun, but it is tied down to the earth. Like the youths and the maidens who feel in themselves the passion of another existence, it is fettered, laid as it were in a grave, and yet with all the fervent desire to arise and to free itself.

IV

WITH the "Songs of Innocence" and most of the "Songs of Experience" closes what we might call Blake's purely poetic period. His mind, after the production of those poems, became filled ever more and more with symbolic theories. The visions of his early years returned to him with renewed vigour, and he peopled for himself a world of beings, half gods, half elemental forces that guide and sway our lives. In 1789, too, came the French Revolution, and the ideas arising out of the French Revolution, combined with his mystic philosophy, were to drive him effectually from the childhood realms of his earlier verse.

In Blake's later years, it is true, he denied politics, thought more of visionary than of actual conditions in a life which he came to regard as worse than death, but it is refreshing to find him, in his earlier years, an enthusiast who could leave his colours and his plates to mingle with men and share their sorrows, their aspirations, and their desires. It is allowed to the aged to seek seclusion in art reverie, but not to the youthful of heart or of body. William Blake was not the man to stand idle when any injustice, or what he thought was injustice, was around him. He was too fiery to remain a passive onlooker at any great event in progress near. He was a passionate enthusiast for the French Revolution, and when even the Mary Wollstonecraft and William Godwin circle he met at the publisher Johnson's were afraid to voice their ideals too openly, he risked lynching by wearing a cap of liberty on his head and by styling himself everywhere a son of the Revolution. His fine verses in "The French Revolution"[9] were inspired and inflamed by the events he saw developing on the Continent.

---

[9] See page 68.

THE FRENCH REVOLUTION

For the Commons convene in the Hall of the Nation. France shakes! And the heavens of France
Perplex'd vibrate round each careful countenance! Darkness of old times around them
Utters loud despair, shadowing Paris; her grey towers groan, and the Bastille trembles.
In its terrible towers the Governor stood, in dark fogs list'ning the horror;
A thousand his soldiers, old veterans of France, breathing red clouds of power and dominion.
Sudden seiz'd with howlings, despair, and black night, he stalk'd like a lion from tower
To tower; his howlings were heard in the Louvre; from court to court restless he dragg'd
His strong limbs; from court to court curs'd the fierce torment unquell'd,
Howling and giving the dark command; in his soul stood the purple plague,
Tugging his iron manacles, and piercing thro' the seven towers dark and sickly,
Panting over the prisoners like a wolf gorg'd. And the den nam'd Horror held a man
Chain'd hand and foot; round his neck an iron band, bound to the impregnable wall;
In his soul was the serpent coil'd round in his heart, hid from the light, as in a cleft rock:
And the man was confin'd for a writing prophetic. In the tower nam'd Darkness was a man
Pinion'd down to the stone floor, his strong bones scarce cover'd with sinews; the iron rings
Were forg'd smaller as the flesh decay'd; a mask of iron on his face hid the lineaments
Of ancient Kings, and the frown of the eternal lion was hid from the oppressed earth.

> But the dens shook and trembled: the prisoners look up and assay to shout; they listen,
> Then laugh in the dismal den, then are silent; and a light walks round the dark towers.
> For the Commons convene in the Hall of the Nation; like spirits of fire in the beautiful
> Porches of the Sun, to plant beauty in the desert craving abyss, they gleam
> On the anxious city: all children new-born first behold them, tears are fled,
> And they nestle in earth-breathing bosoms. So the city of Paris, their wives and children,
> Look up to the morning Senate, and visions of sorrow leave pensive streets.

Earlier than the French Revolution, however, Blake had been in a scene of popular uprising. In 1780, arising out of the Gordon Riots, a vast concourse of people, a howling, shouting mob, attacked the infamous prison of Newgate, broke down its barriers, and liberated the convicts within. Gilchrist[10] tells us that Blake was caught in the surging mass and carried forward in its front rank to witness the destruction of the prison. Now, in the first place, one can generally escape from a crowd if one particularly wants to do so, and, secondly, one certainly does not need to stay in the vanguard of a triumphant mob unless one keeps there by one's own exertions. Blake had very probably more to do with the breaking of the great walls of Newgate–"Stones of Law," as we shall find he called them later–than Gilchrist will confess or knew of. One can almost aver, from knowledge of his character, that he was not a passive onlooker, in any case.

In particular circumstances, we know, he was not inclined to remain still. In 1792 he warned Paine, who had just published the second volume of his "Rights of Man," to flee to France. Paine accepted the advice and managed to escape the English police by twenty minutes. In the same year Blake defended a poor circus boy ill-treated by his master. Blake was then at 28 Poland Street, whither he had removed from his now abandoned print-shop, and Astley's

---

[10] A. Gilchrist, "The Life of William Blake."

Circus was occupying an adjoining piece of ground. The sight that drew forth Blake's indignation was a boy hobbling about with a log of wood chained to his leg—a punishment for misbehaviour. The poet's temper—never too tranquil—instantly fired. He went over straightway, found the master absent, harangued a crowd of circus attendants, and got the boy set loose. In an hour's time Mr Astley himself arrived at Blake's door and was ushered in by the trembling Mrs Blake. The two men almost came to blows, but thanks to Blake's eloquence or to his manner or to his conviction—probably to all three—when the time came for the proprietor to depart he did so in all goodwill and in terms of respect and friendship. Blake had carried his point.

Such are the most notable records of Blake's actual "defence of the distressed," and probably the most interesting of them all, although the saving of Tom Paine has a far greater historical importance, was this latter case of freeing a boy from a species of slavish torture. We seem nearer to Blake after reading that: we seem nearer, too, to a true understanding of his poems.

All through Blake's writings are scattered his belief in freedom, his hatred of oppression and of misery capable of being alleviated, his social and political outbursts. In the narrow sense of the word, of course, politics did not interest Blake one straw. He disregarded demagogues as much as he ignored the Houses of Parliament. His utterances are all raised above the mere party partisanship which distinguishes ordinary politics. There is one thing, however, which must never be lost sight of in any examination of Blake's ideas, and that is, the peculiar way in which personal, social, and visionary theories became mingled in his philosophy. What he held in contempt as a man he condemned in social life, and condemned, too, its manifestations in afterworlds of his imagination. These three elements, or planes, can be observed in all his ideas, from the most general to the most detailed. Blake, for instance, was a philosophic revolutionary: and his revolutionary enthusiasm took the three forms, of personal redressing of wrongs, of social ideals, and of moral principles which plunged deep into man's religious and supermundane instincts and beliefs. He was an artist who painted in an individual manner, who desired all men artists, and who came to look upon every beautiful idea as a manifestation of the æsthetically creative principle of the universe.

In art, naturally, we find the source of all Blake's power and strength. Every single fibre of him thrilled with the creative instinct. Religion, politics, everything assumed for him the hue and the tenour of art. Jesus thus became for him the supreme artist-type who received the spirit of inspiration in the form of the Holy Ghost. His apostles were, in Blake's own words, "all artists." Even when he painted "The Last Judgment" that event became a thing, not of sinners or of saints, but of artists and of philistines. "Thus," he says, "my picture is a history of art and science, the foundation of society, which is Humanity itself. What are the gifts of the Spirit but mental gifts? When any individual rejects error and embraces truth, a Last Judgment passes upon that individual." Bonaparte, and "whomsoever it may concern," he reminds "that it is not the arts that follow and attend upon Empire, but Empire that attends upon and follows arts." He believed that our public buildings should be decorated so that England might become what Italy is–"an envied storehouse of intellectual riches." He wove, as we have already seen, his poems into harmonies of illustrative form and colour: and seemed to desire our daily life to be brightened by the continual observance of beautiful things. His hero in the later mythic prophecies was Los, the spirit of inspiring and inspired poetry, whose task it was at the last day to arouse the slumbrous form of mankind by the fires and the furies of his emotion.

Two other main tendencies of Blake's mind—tendencies which are also of prime importance for an understanding both of his character and of his philosophy—have already been considered. Those two tendencies we have called individualism and antinomianism or anarchy. Not that Blake was an individualist in the lower sense of the word, as applied to a man who desires for himself all the riches of the world and lets the rest go starve. Never affluent in the very least way, he died in a small room at Fountain Court, Strand, with barely an unbroken chair in it, a room, however, which Palmer declares was made by his geniality and his genius "more attractive than the threshold of princes." Blake demanded nothing for himself but liberty, and that he gave freely to every one else. He was an antinomian, a disbeliever in rules, in contrast to an egoist who thinks only of himself. Blake's only hatreds were for those who hindered the development of others. He hated his later patron Hayley, because Hayley had tried to drag him away from the manifestations of his own imagination and fetter him to the wheel of classic imitation. He hated Reynolds because Reynolds would have forced young students to learn and to follow rules that Blake despised. He hated the works of Le Brun and

Rubens, because they seduced the free imagination into realms of petty trivialities. The three Furies in his "Last Judgment" are men whom "the spectator may suppose ... clergymen in the pulpit, scourging sin instead of forgiving it."

Blake desired nothing but liberty to see and to describe his visions, to trace his own way unaided. Those who called him 'madman' had set themselves on pinnacles of conceited sanity which made them into accusers and tyrants. Blake never considered himself peculiar in his visions. Every one, he thought, could have the same if he were not maltreated with false education in his youth. Every man could thus be a judge of art, he deemed, if he had not been "connoisseured out of his senses," and it is on the "connoisseurs" that all his fury falls. For every one else he has infinite pity and love. "A Last Judgment," he says, "is not for the purpose of making bad men better, but of hindering them from oppressing the good," and again, "Forgiveness of sin is only at the judgment seat of Jesus the Saviour [who was, it must be remembered, for Blake the Spirit of Art], where the accuser is cast out, not because he sins, but because he torments the just, and makes them do what he considers as sin and what he knows is opposite to their own identity."

To avoid the necessity of the condemnation of sin itself, Blake formulated the idea of personalities passing through various states, from one of which they pass to another in retrogression or in progress. It is to these "states," he tells us in "Jerusalem," that sin must be imputed, never to individuals. To impute error to individuals was, for Blake, the error of Satan who, neglecting the truth of forgiveness, proscribes individuals who have, in certain states, committed sin. The true attitude then for Blake is the attitude of the man who ignores altogether the failures and the shortcomings of others, and who allows them to work out their own salvation. "It is not," he tells us in 1810, "because angels are holier than men or devils that makes them angels, but because they do not expect holiness from one another, but from God only." To the height of this ideal only one man attained—Christ Himself when He turned from a woman of a thousand sins the revilings of His companions. It sometimes seems to us as almost marvellous how Blake escaped from the wholesale condemnation of Christianity to which Paine and Shelley succumbed. Instead, it is one of the greatest proofs of his intellectual clarity that Blake could distinguish so definitely between the Churches and the religion of

Christ. Shelley, for a time at least, could not do so, but saw only misery and degradation in the exquisitely beautiful ideals of the greatest poet and dreamer who has ever lived. Blake is of the company of the Apostles, nearer to the Central Figure than all of them, save perchance John of the Evangel. Those who, in his own days and in ours, reviled or revile him were reviling the spirit of Christ.

Among the humble, Blake was humble, among the proud, proud. He could hang on children's laughter, watch with those beaming eyes of his the most delicate shadows of lovely things, but he could rise also, in the face of opposition or of contempt, to the highest levels of righteous indignation and of disdain. One knows how he slashed down the impertinent critic of Fuseli in "The Monthly Review" of 1806. Of Sir Thomas Lawrence and all who, in confidential circles, discussed him and said what a pity it was he was mad, he cried "They pity me, but 'tis they are the just objects of pity. I possess my visions and my peace. They have bartered their birth right for a mess of pottage," while in one other magnificent and grandiloquent passage he out-Heroded Herod in his glory. "Can I speak with too great contempt of such fellows?" he asked, speaking again of English connoisseurs. "If all the princes in Europe like Louis IV and Charles I were to patronize such blockheads, I, William Blake, a mental prince, would decollate and hang their souls as guilty of mental high treason."

Blake's ideas in politics have been but little reproduced, and almost the only instance of what may be called 'international theories' is to be found as a marginal note to the poet's copy of Bacon's works. The dictum that caught Blake's attention was the one where the philosopher declares that "the increase of a state must be upon a foreigner." It was one of those authoritative statements, so cruel in its reasoning chill, which made Blake's anger fire out of very contrariness. His answer was one we still have to consider. "The increase," he says, "of a state, as of a man, is from internal improvement or intellectual acquirement. Man is improved not by the hurt of another. States are not improved at the expense of foreigners."

We may be able to pick out a few other similar political dicta in his works or, more probably, in his marginal annotations to works that he had read, but Blake knew that social as well as personal regeneration was to be sought, not by means of Acts of Parliament, but by individual and inner changes in men's hearts. Yet who better than he realized how daily, drudging toil for a livelihood impaired the movement of all intellectual and emotional thought? He saw the tragedy written in the lives of those poor children who "on a Holy Thursday" marched, two and two, in prim universalized uniforms, to sing "trembling cries" before their "cold and usurious" benefactors. He saw the horrible existence of men who toil, year in, year out, for ten or twelve hours a day, to keep bread in their mouths, and who have no time to stir their minds to anything higher than the most brutal of pleasures. He saw the hideous luxury of the rich and their miserly charity doled out in pittances to the poor:

> They compell the Poor to live upon a crust of
>   bread by soft mild arts:
> They reduce the Man to want, then give with
>   pomp and ceremony.
> The praise of Jehovah is chaunted from lips of
>   hunger and thirst.

Although these lines have a more than half symbolic reference to eternal things, as all Blake's words have, they refer too to literal fact. We shall find, when we turn again to his actual works, that there are many of his finest passages inspired by a realization of the misery of the poor and the oppressed, but everywhere we shall find the same phenomenon, the inter-relation and interdependence of the personal, social, and symbolic motives. The vision in "America,"[11] for example, of liberated slaves arising from their fetters, unable to credit the truth of their new fortune, believing it all but a cruel dream which will vanish when waking comes, has a symbolic reference to a liberated mankind, but at the same time it cannot be dissociated from the chains that Blake with his own eyes saw shattered in the fall of Newgate in 1780. It is because of this that a knowledge of Blake's character and of the main events in his life is of so much importance to us in studying his poetry and his philosophy.

This philosophy of Blake's we may now in brief words enunciate, but first we must notice that it varied slightly from its inception about 1790 to its fuller development about 1800. The commentators on Blake's symbolic system

---

[11] See page 74.

have almost always treated it as a formed whole, unchanged from decade to decade. Messrs Ellis and Yeats, and even M. Berger, have dealt with his ideas in this way, not realizing that for Blake, as for Ruskin, "the man who never alters his opinions is like standing water, and breeds reptiles of the mind." From the very first to the very last the forms of Blake's symbolic message were changing. The only three ideas that remained steadfast were those three initial ones we saw running through all his work—art, individuality, brotherhood (and in brotherhood we may include the spirit of freedom). All else of his ideas altered as his life altered from youth to age.

A characteristic instance of this is to be seen in the attitude he assumes toward angels and devils. In 1790, when he was fresh from a critical reading of Swedenborg, he developed a theory that angels had to do with restrictive reason: that Hell had to do with energy and with the fires of the poetic genius. In 1794 this idea was still in his mind, as we can see from the description in "Europe" of the founding of the serpent-temple:

> Image of infinite
> Shut up in finite revolutions, and man become an
> angel,
> Heaven a mighty circle turning: God a tyrant crown'd.

Ten years later, however, in 1804, "Devils" had become "False Religions," while in 1810, as we saw in the passage already quoted,[12] angels were holier than men and devils because they did not expect holiness from one another—that is to say, they were the perfect types of a regenerated humanity.

Such a direct reversal of opinion is to be traced too in his attitude toward human passion. Passion with Blake was always placed in contrast to the restrictive reason, but the crackling fires of "The Marriage of Heaven and Hell" and of the "Visions of the Daughters of Albion" are not by any means the same as the calmer flames of his abnegation theory in the later prophecies.

We cannot, then, describe Blake's symbols for any one period of his activity. They must all be related to his chronological development. Albion in "America" has not the same specialized form as has the Albion of "Jerusalem" or "Milton," just as the other figures borrow new lineaments, change and alter

---

[12] See page 40.

as new ideas fluctuate in his mind. When we enter Blake's symbolic worlds we must remember that we are in a realm of infinite ebb and flow, of elements so ethereal that they melt into one another, change, and reappear as cloud castles do in the azure depths of a summer sky.

In treating of his symbolism, still another fact must be borne in mind, and this system is the least part of Blake's mission of beauty. The system is but the y and the stage-setting for greater, because more important, scenes and portrayals. We must always read between the lines of the 'prophecies' if we are to distil the secret of their true message. There are vast parts of Blake of no interest to anybody but there are others where, beneath the symbolic system, oftentimes so uninviting, lie beauties it is our duty to make one with ourselves, so that we too may become dwellers in the magic realm of sentiment from which they took their birth.

Blake's symbolic system was not a thing artificially manufactured in a short period of time, but was the slow concretization of ideas laid one upon another. This system, as I have indicated, was already foreshadowed in the early "Songs of Innocence" (1789) and in "The Book of Thel" of the same year. In "Tiriel" it develops along a path not followed to any completion. Neither Thel nor Tiriel appears again, and most of the persons of "Tiriel" vanish completely after having been mentioned once in that poem. From the "Visions of the Daughters of Albion" (1793) to "The Book of Ahania" (1795), a system, the precursor of that full development in the three longer 'prophecies,' is enunciated in its simplest and most easily understood phenomena. The imagery of "Vala" (*c.* 1797), of "Jerusalem," and of "Milton (both *c.* 1800 to 1804) is merely an elaboration of the ideas and of the persons hastily sketched in the poems written between 1793 and 1795.

At the risk of being accused of tediousness I shall repeat that the whole of Blake's system takes its rise out of his three main ideas–art, individuality, brotherhood, with liberty surrounding them all as a kind of ineffable grace in eternity, on earth as a burning spirit of infinite revolution, Blake, as we saw, shared the contemporary, new-born faith in progress, but with a reservation— for progress seemed to him rather a retrogression to achieve again virtues which, he believed, had once been in man's possession, but which now were lost. He looked "before and after," seeing a unity and brotherhood in a vague past realm of the Eternals, and viewing it, too, in a future world of regenerated bliss. It is the broken harmony of the present that produces his music and his symbolism, that has given him persons to sing of, revolt to be enjoyed. He is the poet of a shattered mankind.

In man Blake saw a unity, divided by error into a fourfold state: and that fourfold state is applied by him to a multitude of different regions of life and of thought. Man, individually, he divided into *Humanity, Spectre, Emanation,* and *Shadow,* and to these in the staging of eternity corresponded the universalized figures of *Los,* the spirit of imagination and of poetic fire; of *Urizen,* lord of reason and of laws; of *Luvah,* the milder form of spiritual love; and of *Tharmas,* the love that comes from material things. These last four universal essences form the four Zoas, the cardinal, or summarized, part of the Blakean system.

Los, Urizen, Luvah, and Tharmas are the eternal protagonists in Blake's drama of creation and of struggling, tortured life. It is they who require the largest explanation, for in them lies the secret of all Blake's philosophy.

The first of them, *Los,* whose name among the Eternals is Urthona, is the spirit of imaginative life. We have always to remember, of course, the fact we have already noted, that Blake's ideas and creations mingle characteristics taken from his own person, from social life, and from metaphysical reflections. Thus, although Los is the symbol of imagination and impulse in eternity, he becomes identified with other more material figures. In "Milton" and "Jerusalem," for instance, Los becomes identified with that poet whom Blake seems to have admired above all others, as well as with the author himself.

A VISION OF LOS

> While Los heard indistinct in fear, what time I bound my sandals
> On, to walk forward thro' Eternity, Los descended to me:
> And Los behind me stood: a terrible flaming Sun: just close
> Behind my back: I turned round in terror and behold,
> Los stood in that fierce glowing fire; and he also stoop'd down
> And bound my sandals in Udan-Adan: trembling I stood
> Exceedingly with fear and terror, standing in the Vale
> Of Lambeth: but he kissed me and wish'd me health.
> And I became One Man with him arising in my strength:

'Twas too late now to recede. Los had enter'd into my soul:
His terrors now possess'd me whole I arose in fury and strength.

"I am that Shadowy Prophet who Six Thousand Years ago
Fell from my station in the Eternal bosom. Six Thousand Years
Are finish'd. I return both Time and Space obey my will.
I in Six Thousand Years walk up and down: for not one Moment
Of Time is lost, nor one Event of Space unpermanent,
But all remain: every fabric of Six Thousand Years
Remains permanent: tho' on the Earth, where Satan
Fell, and was cut off, all things vanish and are seen no more,
They vanish not from me and mine, we guard them first and last.
The Generations of Men run on in the tide of Time,
But leave their destin'd lineaments permanent for ever."

So spake Los as we went along to his supreme abode.[13]

Elsewhere he even assumed the divine form of Jesus, that Jesus Who, in "The Everlasting Gospel," was regarded as the true artist-type, acting by impulse and not by rule. "Then Jesus appeared standing by Albion," says Blake,

> As the Good Shepherd
> By the lost Sheep that he hath found, and Albion knew that it
> Was the Lord, the Universal Humanity, and Albion saw his Form
> A Man, and they conversed together as Man with Man, in Ages of Eternity.
> And the Divine Appearance was the likeness and similitude of Los.[14]

---

[13] "Milton."
[14] "Jerusalem."

This magnificent creation of Blake has been compared with the Earth Spirit in "Faust" and with the Demogorgon in "Prometheus Unbound," but he has even a greater affinity to the Demon of Carducci's fancy, who heralded the spirit of revolt and of progress in modern Europe. He is the incarnation of that essence among us which, in an age of tyranny, still conveys to man a message of past glories and of faith in progress—the guardian of man's best instincts even when those instincts seem overweighed by misery, forgetfulness, and oppression. Los is the incarnation, not only of poetry, but of constructive antinomianism, revolting in a fallen age, rejoicing in one of happy bliss and liberation. There is a double epos in the narrative doings of Los as it appears in e pages of Blake. In the first—told in "The Book of Urizen" and in "The Book of Los"[15]—he is pointed by the Eternals to watch over the self-abstraction of Urizen, who passes from change to change until he reaches the "limit of contraction" in the human Adam. This epos is a tale of terror and of tragedy for the figure of Los. In it he is merely staying, never revolting or rejoicing. In his later appearances, however, in "Jerusalem" and in "Milton," his mission is changed. There he is the very essence of imaginative life. His anvils ring with the blows of his prophetic strength. He builds the marvellous citadel of Golgonooza—the City of Art—the home of the Golden Age. There Urizen's degeneration has ceased, but his power has grown, and against that power it is Los alone who flings the whole might of his enthusiasm in an endeavour to raise from the fallen, crass materialism of humanity patterns, at least, modelled upon the divine archetypes of which his imagination is full. The acts of the revolutionary are never tragic, no matter to what end they come, save only when they are merely destructive: and neither Blake nor his essence, Los, ever rested wholly on destruction. Creation was to Blake the divine command given to him: and if, in a degenerated age, he had to clear paths ere the foundation of his city could be built, he knew when the pulling down of the old should cease and the raising of the new begin.

Wherever we find creation, there is the power of Los. Even in material things it is he who created men's physical bodies as well as their finest impulses. He is the life-force of the universe. Wherever a new and beautiful thing has to be reformed out of an old and worthless one, there on our cheeks

---

[15] See page 75 ff.

we feel the flare of the furnaces of Los, hear the mighty swing of his hammer, and catch, faint or loud, as the wind carries it to us, the eternal harmony of his song.

THE ANVILS OF LOS

> In Bowlahoola[16] Los's Anvils stand and his Furnaces rage;
> Thundering the Hammers beat, and the Bellows blow loud,
> Living, self-moving, mourning, lamenting, and howling incessantly.
> Bowlahoola thro' all its porches feels, tho' too fast founded,
> Its pillars and porticoes to tremble at the force
> Of mortal or immortal arm; and softly lilling flutes,
> Accordant with the horrid labours, make sweet melody.[17]
> Terrified at the sublime Wonder, Los stood before his Furnaces,
> And they stood around, terrified with admiration at Erin's Spaces,
> For the Spaces reach d from the starry heighth, to the starry depth:
> And they builded Golgonooza: terrible eternal labour![18]

The second of Blake's figures of eternity, as it is the second of his divisions of the individual man, is the spirit of reason, developing in a fallen state into rigid, stony law and repression. In infinity this spirit is called *Urizen*, in individual man he takes the form of the Spectre. "Each man," Blake says, in inverted writing, near a magnificent design on page 41[19] of "Jerusalem,"

> Each man is in his Spectre's power
> Until the arrival of that hour,
> When his Humanity awake
> And cast his Spectre into the lake.

---

[16] Bowlahoola is here evidently used for the world. It is, in Blake's mythology, a place founded by Tharmas where "the Human Vegetated Form" is created.

[17] "Milton."

[18] "Jerusalem."

[19] The reference here and in similar cases later is to Blake's original engraved edition.

Urizen is the Lord of this World, until a future age shall set him, not overthrown but regenerated, into the divine unity of which the souls of men form the individual parts.

Urizen is not entirely the Jupiter of "Prometheus Unbound," with whom he has been compared, but a far less abstract figure. He has a dramatic personality which is lacking in Shelley's conception. Had Blake only concentrated his delineation of him into a smaller and less scattered space, we might now be regarding and quoting Urizen as we do the other great tragic characters who have been a nemesis of fate. The "fatal error" in Urizen's case was des this desire drove him relentlessly on to destruction. Clad in divine intelligence, he immemorial ages ago, in God's bosom, in harmony with the other Eternals, until, in an evil hour, the egoistic doubts and longings began to enter his soul. He wished to rule, to have a separate being of his own.

> Lo, a Shadow of Horror is risen
> In Eternity unknown, unprolific,
> Self-clos'd, all-repelling. What Demon
> Hath form'd this abominable Void,
> This soul-shudd'ring Vacuum? Some said
> It is Urizen. But unknown, abstracted,
> Brooding secret, the dark power hid.
>
> . . . .
>
> Dark, revolving in silent activity,
> Unseen in tormenting passions:
> An Activity unknown and horrible,
> A self-contemplating Shadow,
> In enormous labours occupied.[20]

Such was the start of the career of Urizen: and from that start he passed inevitably from change to change, from abyss to deep abyss, Los, as we saw, still guarding his altering lineaments, powerless to stay but eager to avenge. In the end Urizen remains what we see him in Blake's drama, the lawgiving

---

[20] "The Book of Urizen."

power, who has passed from his own seat of reason and penetrated into the realms of another, the realms of Luvah and of love. From him come all the tyrannies and the self-conscious powers raised as a hindrance over other men. Urizen, in fine, is the foe of and the direct contrast to Los. Where Los praises inspiration and fire and mercy, Urizen writes his "Book of Brass":

THE BRAZEN BOOK OF URIZEN

And Urizen read in his Book of Brass in sounding tones:–
"Listen, O Daughters, to my voice! listen to the words of wisdom!
Compel the Poor to live upon a crust of bread by soft mild arts:
So shall (you) govern over all. Let Moral Duty tune your tongue,
But be your hearts harder than the nether millstone;
To bring the Shadow of Enitharmon beneath our wondrous Tree,[21]
That Los may evaporate like smoke, and be no more.
Smile when they frown, frown when they smile; and when a man
    looks pale
With labour and abstinence, say he looks healthy and happy;
And when his children sicken, let them die: there are enough
Born, even too many, and our earth will soon be overrun
Without these arts. If you would make the Poor live with temper,
With pomp give every crust of bread you give; with gracious
    cunning
Magnify small gifts; reduce the man to want a gift, and then give
    with pomp.
Say he smiles, if you hear him sigh; if pale, say he is ruddy.
Preach temperance: say he is overgorg'd, and drowns his wit
In strong drink, tho' you know that bread and water are all
He can afford. Flatter his wife, pity his children, till we can
Reduce all to our will, as spaniels are taught with art."[22]

The four Zoas of Blake's system are completed in the figures of *Luvah*, and of *Tharmas*, corresponding in the individual man to the *Emanation* and the

---

[21] The Tree of Mystery and of Law.
[22] "Vala."

Shadow. Luvah is the spirit of unearthly love—love in its purest, least passionate sense. The Emanation is man's wife upon earth, the symbol of his gentlest qualities. When divided from the whole man, however, the Emanation either stays as the direct contrast to the Spectre, or it is changed by this "error" of separation, and becomes a figure of jealousy. Luvah, in the same way, is the companion of Los, and yet, in a great part of Blake's works, he appears as an evil force through being driven by Urizen's from his own seat in the Heart to Urizen's rejected seat of the Mind. This changing of "states" is really the cause of half the tragedy in Blake's drama of eternity. Urizen is not evil until he tries to rule in Luvah's province: Luvah is all perfection until he is forced to a region he knows not of and which is alien to his desires. This again is but another way of expressing Blake's personal dislike of "connoisseurs", and all the people who mind businesses other than their own.

A union of Los and of Luvah is to be found in two great figures of the Blakean cycle. These are *Orc* and *Christ*. Orc is the spirit of flaming, passionate love, just as, for Blake, Christ is. Both burn to create a finer universe for man. Both bear within them Blake's doctrine of forgiving, unselfish love. Neither is mild or tender, but flaming and outwith all laws save those of its own imagining. They have in them the purity of altruistic emotion as well as the artist's passion for revolt and for creation. Both batter against the mighty gates of Urizen's brazen citadel. Both act "from impulse and not from rule," and "burn in the fires of Eternal Youth."

Were it not for the creative spirit of Los, Luvah would form the central hero of this drama of infinity: but, as it is, love, although the ultimately triumphant force of the universe, must subordinate itself to the creative antinomianism of revolution, symbolized in the artist in general and in Los in particular.

Tharmas, the last Zoa, is a lower form of love, the spirit of "vegetative" existence, of physical forces, beautiful in innocence, but horrible and brutal when confined by restrictive law or driven into imaginary sin. Tharmas corresponds to the Shadow in man, connected in thought with the "veils" of Vala, the goddess of nature. The Shadow is mere sense perception, not the true vision of reality, and Tharmas is man's physical love.

The two great contending forces in man, as divined by Blake, are the *Spectre* and *Emanation*, the spirit of reason and the spirit of love, both marred and rendered obnoxious when reft out of their proper realms. So, too, each of those four chief protagonists of the more spacial drama have themselves a divided Spectre and Emanation, their spectres usually nameless because evil, and their Emanations, because originally lovely, individually recognized. The chief of all the Emanations is *Jerusalem*, into whom the Emanations of all things will ultimately merge and mingle in one beautiful unity. Jerusalem is the "Emanation of the giant Albion," the typical man. She is "nam'd Liberty among the Sons of Albion," who are men. She is at once a symbol of tender impulse, of loving thought, of natural simplicity, and a symbolic name for a poet's ideal, for a city of the Spirit which represents in itself a perfected type of humanity. Finally, she is the incarnation of the forgiveness of sins. Her drama is wrought out in the longest prophecy of Blake's which is preserved for us.

The other chief Emanations are those of the Four Zoas.

The Emanation of Los is *Enitharmon*, divine pity, as we see her in "The Book of Urizen." On earth, in man's fallen state, she "is the vegetated mortal wife of Los, his Emanation, yet his wife till the sleep of Death is past." In "Jerusalem" and in "Vala" she is, like Jerusalem, the artist's joy, the hovering ideal which flits before man, never attainable, encouraging and denying.

The Emanation of Urizen is *Ahania*, the softest part of his power, but when he descended in his abysmal chaos she became to him a sin, never to be reunited to him until after ages should regenerate his tyrannous qualities. It is her despair at his jealousy and her desire for him that give us the fine lament in the fifth chapter of "The Book of Ahania."[23]

It is the reuniting of those two that gives us that magnificent passage of the Ninth Night of "Vala":

THE REUNION OF URIZEN AND AHANIA

> And lo! like harvest moon, Ahania cast off her dark clothes–
> She folded them up in care, in silence, and her brightening limbs
> Bathed in the clear spring of the rock: then from her darksome cave
> Issued in majesty divine. Urizen rose from his couch
> On wings of tenfold joy, clapping his hands, his radiant wings
> In the immense. As when the sun dances upon the mountains,

---

[23] See pages 79-80.

A shout of jubilee in lovely notes resounds from daughter to daughter,
From son to son, as if the stars beaming innumerable
Through night, should sing soft warbling, filling the earth and heaven,
And bright Ahania took her seat by Urizen in songs and joy.

Vala is the Emanation of Luvah. As Jerusalem is the spirit of mutual forgiveness, the very soul of true womanly love, so Vala is the body of that love. She is beauty, material beauty, and in her Blake symbolized all the manifold forms of nature. "Vala," he declared, "produced the bodies: Jerusalem gave the souls," and all through the later books she appears, now as deceitful beauty, symbolized in the 'veils' of Vala, which reave men away from true love into mere selfish unions of man and of woman, now as natural religion, based on mere sense perception, now as an aider and abetter of Urizen in his laws of false chastity.

To realize Blake's hatred of Vala we must appreciate first of all his true and intense love of all natural things when seen in the light of eternity,[24] and secondly, we must remember his belief that physical phenomena, deprived of that eternal radiance, "obliterate imagination." He adored physical beauty, and yet he realized that that beauty dimmed a higher loveliness of the soul. By viewing Vala he forgot Jerusalem. "Why wilt thou give," he cried to her concerning Jerusalem, "why wilt thou give to her a body whose life is but a Shade?" In those words Blake's philosophy may be seen enshrined–his hatred of vegetative life and his dependence upon it.

The Emanation of Tharmas is a much more shadowy one, *Enion* by name, symbol of purely generative emotions, as Tharmas is of physical ones. Yet for Blake she is not entirely evil. Neither Tharmas nor Enion has, in his mind, the subtlety and the deceit of Vala. They are rather symbols of that

Infancy, fearless, lustful, happy, nestling for delight
In laps of pleasure! Innocence, honest, open, seeking
The vigorous joys of morning light. ...[25]

---

[24] See pages 14-15.
[25] "Visions of the Daughters of Albion."

It is Tharmas who awakes America: and in "Vala" we find Enion united with him again, both appearing as "two little children playing ... beneath the trees ... in an eternal childhood." Tharmas struggles with Los—yes, as physical emotions struggle with higher ones but, at the same time, in Blake's philosophy, the physical emotions, when unrestricted, keep alive, in an otherwise unpoetic and unredeemed section of humanity, glimmerings of eternity and of revolt.

To most of the Four Zoas Blake apportioned a plentiful progeny: but the majority of their names are too unimportant to receive more than scant mention here. In the "Visions of the Daughters of Albion," for instance, we come across Theotormon and Bromion, both sons of Los and Enitharmon, and who, with Rintrah and Palambron, make up another fourfold system of West, North, South, and East, corresponding in yet another way to Tharmas, Los, Urizen, and Luvah. The scattered passages in which Blake connects the numerous parts of this system are many, and extend from the design on page 32 of "Milton" to the interpretative passage on page 12 of "Jerusalem." In the design of "Milton" Blake sketches out the four worlds—North, South, East, and West—belonging to Urthona (Los), Urizen, Luvah, and Tharmas, while in "Jerusalem" he tells us that "fourfold are the Sons of Los in their divisions," where "the Four Points are thus beheld in Great Eternity: the West, the Circumference: South, the Zenith: North, the Nadir: East, the Centre unapproachable for ever. ... And the Eyes are the South, and the Nostrils are the East, and the Tongue is the West, and the Eat is the North." When one collects all those little snatches of explanation which Blake has placed in the midst of his prophecies, his whole system, allowing for the chronological development we have already noted, seems wonderfully unified, and may be placed down in definite tabulated form. (see page 55)

When one knows the tabula of names given in this list, and when one keeps in remembrance the general trend of his ideas, including his habit of splitting everything up into fours, one in reality knows sufficient to be able to read the greater part of Blake's symbolic utterances. The value of knowing this philosophic system of his, even for the reading of what seem like simple lyrics, could not be better illustrated than by taking the "Motto" from "The Book of Thel":

> Does the Eagle know what is in the pit
> Or wilt thou go ask the Mole?
> Can Wisdom be put in a silver rod,
> Or Love in a golden bowl?

On the outside that seems a fairly simple little four-verse stanza, but if one refers to the tabula opposite one will find that silver is the metal of the East, of Luvah and of Love, whereas gold is the metal of the South, of Urizen and of Reason. What Blake means to say, then, is: Can Wisdom be compressed into the region of the emotions and of love, or can Love be transferred from its own realm into the realm of the understanding? Unless we know at least a fragment of the system the full meaning of this and of other works of Blake cannot possibly be fathomed.

SUMMARY OF BLAKE'S FOURFOLD SYSTEM

	North	*South*	*East*	*West*
Compass Points:				
Zoas	Los	Urizen	Luvah	Tharmas
Emanation of Zoas	Enitharmon	Ahania	Vala	Enion
Sons of Los	Bromion	Rintrah	Palambron	Theotormon
Parts of Spiritual Man	Humanity	Spectre	Emanation	Shadow
Points in Eternity	Nadir	Zenith	Centre	Circumference
Directions	Breadth	Height	Inward	Outward
Parts of Man	Womb	Head	Heart	Lions
Senses	Ear	Eyes	Nostrils	Tongue
Towns	Edinburgh (N.)	Verulam (S.)	London (E.)	York (W.)
Metals	Iron	Gold	Silver	Brass
Spiritual States	Eden	Generation	Beulah	Ulro
Arts	Architecture	Poetry	Music	Painting
Elements	Earth	Fire	Air	Water
Spirits	Gnomes	Fairies	Genii	Nymphs
Emotions	Wrath Vision	Reason Intellect	Mercy Love	Desire Instinct

A closer knowledge of Blake's other shifting and vanishing figures is quite unnecessary for any appreciative reader, who may, if he so desires, skip many a passage of dreary and detailed enumeration. The only persons of real importance are the Zoas and their Emanations, together with the 'giant' Albion and his Emanation, Jerusalem. In the "Visions of the Daughters of Albion," for instance, we do not even need to know the genealogy of the principal figures, Theotormon and Bromion. There, they are characters sufficiently individualized to charm our intellect with their own personalities. Thel explains herself, and so, indeed, does every other character of any con sequence whom Blake has introduced into this drama of universal humanity. There are the sons and the daughters of Los, for example, of whom the most important are Rahab, the harlot, who is another form of Vala in her aspect of law-giving religion, and Tirzah, whom we have already noted in the "Songs of Experience," as the essence of motherhood. Again, there are the sons of Urizen, classed, like their father, among the reasoners and the proud, or the sons of Albion, with names, most of them, taken from men whom Blake himself knew. Skofield, one of the worst of these, was the name of a soldier enemy at Felpham.[26] The daughters of Albion have also names peculiar in Blakean symbolism, these names being taken mostly from romance or Shakespearean plays—Cordella, Ignoge, Gonorill, Sabrina, and Ragan—names only half disguised from their Miltonic or Shakespearean originals. All of these, however, are unimportant, or interpreted in the passages where they occur.

Even the names of those countries where his soul characters dwelt need not be learned by heart. The scene of Blake's eternal drama is, after all, in the mind of man. When we hear of Los at his hammers we picture around him no special surroundings. His furnace fires dim all. The persons of his drama needed no background, and Blake gave them none. What he saw, he saw intensified, all the surrounding details lost in a shadowy haze. When we read, then, of strangely-sounding cities and lands, we must imagine only spiritual states, invisible because being only moods of the infinite spirit of man. Even the detailed city of art, Golgonooza, in "Jerusalem," stands hung in space, with gates opening on nowhere, a city, carefully described as are its most minute particulars, as ideal and as intangible as the most visionary of his aerial spaces.

---

[26] See page 89.

Four alone of those lands are important, and those solely because they recur fairly often in Blake's works. These are Beulah, Entuthon Benython, Udan Adan, and Ulro. *Beulah* is the "land of shades," a vision of blessedness:

> There is from great Eternity a mild and pleasant rest
> Named Beulah, a soft moony universe, feminine, lovely,
> Pure, mild and gentle[27]

Entuthon Benython is the land of abstract philosophy:

> A dark and unknown night, indefinable, immeasurable,
>   without end,
> Abstract Philosophy warring in enmity against Imagination.[28]

Near it, or on it, is the terrible lake of *Udan Adan*, the sphere of indefiniteness—Blake's greatest dread, for he, like Dante, abhorred hazy outlines. It is

> A lake not of waters but of spaces
> Perturbed, black and deadly.
>
> Formed of the tears and sighs and death sweat of the
>   victims
> Of Urizen's Laws, to irrigate the roots of the tree of
>   Mystery.[29]

Ulro "is the space of the terrible starry wheels of Albion's sons"—a world of sleep and of inactivity, a world of degradation and of sorrow, where man is reft of hope and of light, cast as in a lotus-dream of weary lassitude.

Such, then, are the main points of his system. We may trace character in Blake's tiniest, most insignificant characters, but these are always overshadowed by the vast and predominant forces around them. Because he loved detail so much, I believe that we, to gain the fullest appreciation of him,

---

[27] "Vala."
[28] "Jerusalem."
[29] "Vala."

must concentrate on central effect, counterbalancing so the exaggerated tendency of his mind. We must, at least, endeavour to gather together from the scattered notices the outstanding features of his myth: and to do that briefly has been my aim in the preceding few pages. We need not stay at the details. It is the misfortune of Blake that where he most elaborated, there his poetry fails, but it is his triumph that so little in reality do we need to pause over his fictitious names—that we can pass so easily and so profitably into a world of pure poetry and of exalted emotion which dilates our spirits and fills our hearts with the sentiment of eternity.

V

TEDIOUS as the enumeration, bereft of the poetry, may appear, this account of Blake's main theories is made absolutely essential by the fact that every work of his after 1789 has in it a mass of symbolic material. The first group of these, connected intimately with the "Songs of Innocence and of Experience," consists of many of the multitudinous shorter poems contained in the Rossetti and Pickering manuscripts, "Tiriel" (written about 1788-9), "The Book of Thel" (engraved 1789), and "The Marriage of Heaven and Hell" (engraved 1790). Closely connected with the last mentioned work is "The French Revolution" (set in type 1791).

All this time Blake was residing at 28 Poland Street, meeting, as I have shown, a number of philosophic revolutionaries at the publisher Johnson's, flaunting his red cap of liberty, alternately brooding over his mystical theories and flaring with revolutionary passion. "Tiriel and "Thel" are the expressions of the mystical meditations; "The Marriage of Heaven and Hell," with "The French Revolution," shows us the revolutionary enthusiast.

"Thel," engraved in the same year as the "Songs of Innocence," is the poem most nearly connected with the earlier group. It is a marvel of art—a marvel of sweetly sought words and of limpid measure, of delicate colours and of harmonious line. It is possibly the most purely beautiful thing that Blake ever produced.

It introduced too, for the first time, if we preclude the undated and possibly earlier "Tiriel," Blake's unique metrical measure—a long seven-foot line consisting mainly of trochees. This became in time his normal measure, the measure which, "with a variety in every line," developed into something which, for him, was entirely different from and greater than the "monotonous cadence like that used by Milton and Shakespeare ... derived from the modern bondage of rhyming."

Concerning this measure opinions differ, some, like Mr Ellis, claiming for it future glory, and others, like Professor Saintsbury, inclined to regard the most of it as mere rhythmical prose. In places, certainly, we must confess that the lines are prose, and often bad prose at that, yet notwithstanding those arid passages in "Milton" and in "Jerusalem," Blake's measure, as employed by him, displays a million beauties of rhythm and of poetic ingenuity. In his hands it betrays some of the suppleness and adaptability which our blank verse has done in the hands of our finest poets. With Blake it can be either terrible and awe-inspiring or gentle as the flowers of innocence. In "Jerusalem" he can exclaim in lamenting tones:

> O I am nothing when I enter into judgment with thee!
> If thou withdraw thy breath I die and vanish into Hades,
> If thou dost lay thine hand upon me, behold I am silent:
> If thou withhold thine hand, I perish like a fallen leaf.
> O I am nothing: and to nothing must return again:
> If thou withdraw thy breath, Behold, I am oblivion.

Or, changing the rhythm, he can thunder forth words of revolt and of horror:

> Then the ancientest Peer, Duke of Burgundy, rose from the
>   Monarch's right hand, red as wines
> From his mountains; an odour of war, like a ripe vineyard,
>   rose from his garments,
> And the chamber became as a clouded sky; o'er the Council
>   he stretch'd his red limbs
> Cloth'd in flames of crimson: as a ripe vineyard stretches over
>   sheaves of corn,
> The fierce Duke hung over the Council: around him crowd,
>   weeping in his burning robe,
> A bright cloud of infant souls his words fall like purple
>   autumn on the sheaves.[30]

"The Book of Thel" displays this metre used for gentle things, and the "mild song" found therein flows with an even movement, reminding us of the soft ripple of a summer stream. As this "Book of Thel" is one of the shortest,

---

[30] "The French Revolution."

and at the same time one of the most easily understood of Blake's prophetic works, I shall give it here in full. In reading it we must remember Blake's study of Swedenborg. Apparently Thel is at first an innocent soul about to be born into this mortal world (which for Blake at this time was death). Then she laments at the transitoriness of all joy and is comforted by various lowly and humble things—by the Lily of the Valley (ll. 19-47), by a Cloud (ll. 48-78), by a Worm (ll. 49-84), and finally by a Clod of Clay (ll. 85-107). Clay is the material of our mortal bodies, and Thel wanders to her own grave-plot (her body to be) and listens to the voice of lamentation there. It is the poetry of this work, however, and not its symbolic content, that charms our sense. Its beauty is perfect. It is, indeed, what M. Berger calls it, one of the most beautiful elegies in the whole range of human poetry.

THE BOOK OF THEL

Thel's Motto

Does the Eagle know what is in the pit
Or wilt thou go ask the Mole?
Can Wisdom be put in a silver rod,
Or Love in a golden bowl?

I

The daughters of the Seraphim led round their sunny flocks–
All but the youngest: she in paleness sought the secret air,
To fade away like morning beauty from her mortal day:
Down by the river of Adona her soft voice is heard,
And thus her gentle lamentation falls like morning dew:–

"O life of this our spring! why fades the lotus of the water?
Why fade these children of the spring, born but to smile and
   fall?
Ah! Thel is like a wat'ry bow, and like a parting cloud;
Like a reflection in a glass; like shadows in the water;
Like dreams of infants, like a smile upon an infant's face;
Like the dove's voice; like transient day; like music in the air.

Ah! gentle may I lay me down, and gentle rest my head,
And gentle sleep the sleep of death, and gentle hear the voice
Of Him that walketh in the garden in the evening time!"

The Lily of the Valley, breathing in the humble grass,
Answered the lovely maid and said: "I am a wat'ry weed,
And I am very small, and love to dwell in lowly vales;
So weak, the gilded butterfly scarce perches on my head.
Yet I am visited from heaven; and He that smiles on all,
Walks in the valley, and each morn over me spreads His hand,
Saying, 'Rejoice, thou humble grass, thou new-
born lily-flower,
Thou gentle maid of silent valleys and of modest brooks;
For thou shalt be clothed in light, and fed with morning
 manna,
Till summer's heat melts thee beside the fountains and the
 springs,
To flourish in eternal vales.' Then why should
Thel complain?
Why should the mistress of the vales of Her utter a sigh?"

She ceas'd, and smil'd in tears, then sat down in her silver
 shrine.

Thel answer'd: "O thou little Virgin of the peaceful valley,
Giving to those that cannot crave, the voiceless, the o'ertired;
Thy breath doth nourish the innocent lamb; he smells thy
 milky garments,
He crops thy flowers, while thou sittest smiling in his face,
Wiping his mild and meeking mouth from all contagious
 taints.
Thy wine doth purify the golden honey; thy per-
fume,
Which thou dost scatter on every little blade of grass that
 springs,
Revives the milked cow, and tames the fire-breathing steed.

But Thel is like a faint cloud kindled at the rising sun:
I vanish from my pearly throne, and who shall find my place?"

"Queen of the vales," the Lily answer'd, "ask the tender
    Cloud,
And it shall tell thee why it glitters in the morning sky,
And why it scatters its bright beauty thro' the humid air.
Descend, O little Cloud, and hover before the eyes of Thel."
The Cloud descended, and the Lily bowed her modest head,
And went to mind her numerous charge among the verdant
    grass.

II

"O little Cloud," the Virgin said, "I charge thee tell to me
Why thou complainest not, when in one hour thou fade
    away:
Then we shall seek thee, but not find. Ah! Thel is like to thee:
I pass away: yet I complain, and no one hears my voice."

The Cloud then show'd his golden head and his bright form
    emerg'd,
Hovering and glittering on the air before the face of Thel.

"O Virgin, know'st thou not our steeds drink of the golden
    springs
Where Luvah doth renew his horses? Look'st thou on my
    youth,
And fearest thou, because I vanish and am seen no more,
Nothing remains? O Maid, I tell thee, when I pass away,
It is to tenfold life, to love, to peace, to raptures holy.
Unseen descending, weigh my light wings upon balmy
    flowers,
And court the fair-eyed dew, to take me to her shining tent:
The weeping virgin, trembling, kneels before the risen sun,

Till we arise, link'd in a golden band, and never part.
But walk united, bearing food to all our tender flowers."

"Dost thou, O little Cloud? I fear I am not like thee,
For I walk thro' the vales of Har, and smell the sweetest flowers,
But I feed not the little flowers; I hear the warbling birds,
But I feed not the warbling birds; they fly and seek their food.
But Thel delights in these no more, because I fade away;
And all shall say, 'Without a use this shining woman liv'd,
Or did she only live to be at death the food of worms?'"

The Cloud reclin'd upon his airy throne, and answer'd thus:—

"Then if thou art the food of worms, O Virgin of the skies,
How great thy use, how great thy blessing!
Everything that lives
Lives not alone nor for itself. Fear not, and I will call
The weak Worm from its lowly bed, and thou shalt hear its voice.
Come forth, Worm of the silent valley, to thy pensive Queen."

The helpless Worm arose, and sat upon the Lily's leaf,
And the bright Cloud sail'd on, to find his partner in the vale.

III

Then Thel, astonish'd, view'd the Worm upon its dewy bed.

"Art thou a Worm? Image of weakness, art thou but a Worm?
I see thee like an infant wrapped in the Lily's leaf.
Ah weep not, little voice; thou canst not 'speak,
but thou canst weep.
Is this a Worm? I see thee lay helpless and naked, weeping,
And none to answer, none to cherish thee with mother's smiles."

The Clod of Clay heard the Worm's voice and rais'd her
    pitying head;
She bow'd over the weeping infant, and her life exhal'd
In milky fondness: then on Thel she fix'd her humble eyes.

"O Beauty of the vales of Har! we live not for ourselves.
Thou seest me, the meanest thing, and so I am indeed.
My bosom of itself is cold, and of itself is dark;
But He, that loves the lowly, pours His oil upon
my head,
And kisses me, and binds His nuptial bands around my breast,
And says: 'Thou mother of my children, I have lovèd thee,
And I have given thee a crown that none can take away.'
But how this is, sweet Maid, I know not, and I cannot know;
I ponder and I cannot ponder; yet I live and love."

The Daughter of Beauty wip'd her pitying tears with her
    white veil,
And said: "Alas! I knew not this, and therefore did I weep.
That God would love a worm I knew, and punish the evil foot
That wilful bruis'd its helpless form; but that he cherish'd it
With milk and oil I never knew, and therefore did I weep;
And I complain'd in the mild air, because I fade away,
And lay me down in thy cold bed, and leave my shining lot."

"Queen of the vales," the matron Clay answer'd,
"I heard thy sighs,
And all thy moans flew o'er my roof, but I have call'd them
    down.
Wilt thou, O Queen, enter my house? 'Tis given thee to enter
And to return: fear nothing, enter with thy virgin feet."

IV

The eternal gates' terrific Porter lifted the northern bar:
Thel enter'd in, and saw the secrets of the land unknown.

She saw the couches of the dead, and where the fibrous root
Of every heart on earth infixes deep its restless twists:
A land of sorrows and of tears where never smile was seen.

She wander'd in the land of clouds thro' valleys dark, list'ning
Dolours and lamentations; waiting oft beside a dewy grave,
She stood in silence, list'ning to the voices of the ground,
Till to her own grave-plot she came, and there she sat down,
And heard this voice of sorrow breathed from the hollow pit.

"Why cannot the Ear be closed to its own destruction?
Or the glist'ning Eye to the poison of a smile?
Why are Eyelids stor'd with arrows ready drawn,
Where a thousand fighting-men in ambush lie,
Or an Eye of gifts and graces show'ring fruits and coinèd gold?
Why a Tongue impress'd with honey from every wind?
Why an Ear, a whirlpool fierce to draw creations in?
Why a Nostril wide inhaling terror, trembling, and affright?
Why a tender curb upon the youthful burning boy?
Why a little curtain of flesh on the bed of our desire?"

The Virgin started from her seat, and with a shriek
Fled back unhinder'd till she came into the vales of Har.

After "Thel," it must be confessed that its companion poem, "Tiriel," is, as a work of art, a failure. Its symbolism is confused and the measure and the wording are prosaic and weak. The year after engraving "Thel," however, Blake, in the fulness of his revolutionary enthusiasm, wrote the first of those half-dozen books of his which take their rise from the outbreak of civil disturbance in France. "The Marriage of Heaven and Hell" is almost, we might say, the direct antithesis to "The Book of Thel," bearing within it, as it does, all the fires and the fury of experience. It is not a single poem, but a series of passages in verse and in prose, united by a common faith and enthusiasm. It is a defence of that Hell (the home of impulse) which arises from Evil, which is, in Blake's words, "the active springing from Energy." Evil is set here in direct contraposition to Blake's hated Good, "the passive that obeys Reason."

We cannot understand this poem at all unless we understand this complete topsy-turvyism of ideas and names. Life is death (the birth into spiritual freedom), death is mortal existence (the death of the spirit), Hell is Blake's heaven, and Heaven is the abode of Urizen, the tyrant god who imposes his own selfish rules upon others. "Energy," cried Blake, "is Eternal Delight. ... Those who restrain Desire, do so because theirs is weak enough to be restrained: and the restrainer or Reason usurps its place and governs the unwilling." The whole book, then, celebrating energy, is one long passionate defence of poetic vision, one long denunciation of dull analytics and of systematic reasoning. The "Memorable Fancies" contained in it all repeat in symbolic language the same message. His friends are Devils, his enemies are Angels (representatives of analytic philosophy). He has read Milton and found that he was "of the Devil's party without knowing it." Milton too, as a poet, was on the side of impulse, but, constrained by his age, put the God of Reason, the Jehovah, where Satan should have been. Besides the "Memorable Fancies" which make up the greater part of this work, the most interesting and valuable things in it are the "Proverbs of Hell," retailed by Blake to show the nature of "Infernal Wisdom."

"The road of excess leads to the palace of wisdom," he begins, as an apology for his own methods of creating. "Exuberance is beauty," he cries again, and "Improvement makes straight roads, but the crooked roads without improvement are roads of Genius." These epigrams or 'proverbs' are in their own way marvels of thought: they may be exaggerated because of the coldness of the world around him, but they are the concentrated essence of years of emotion and of meditation. They are the symbolic presentation of his larger message. Let us take an example. "Prisons are built with stones of Law, brothels with bricks of Religion." To explain this one sentence one would require several pages of commentary to display how Blake believed that sin came from restrictive law, evil from bounding and fettering creeds. Already, in the "Songs of Experience," his Garden of Love had become desolate by reason of a Chapel built in its midst, with "Thou shalt not" written over its door:

> And I saw it was filled with graves,
> And tomb-stones where flowers should be;
> And priests in black gowns were walking their rounds,
> And binding with briers my joys and desires.

For him by this time freedom had become the only verity. Law, he but created theft and murder and ugliness, restrictive religion the brothels that would disappear were liberty to come once again to a regenerated humanity. From these proverbs the critic of Blake's work may receive a plentiful store of interpretation. "What is now prov'd was once only imagin'd," "One thought fills immensity," "To create a little flower is the labour of ages." Listening to these words we come nearer to the mystical soul of Blake himself, that Blake whose deepening and inspired eyes gaze forward from the Tatham portrait or search into ours in the painting of Phillips.

In 1791, when all men's minds were turned to the strange, overwhelming events on the Continent, the publisher Johnson set up in type the first part of a long epic by Blake entitled "The French Revolution: A Poem, in Seven Books." That this work was ever really put on the market is extremely improbable, and, until four years ago, every trace of it had disappeared. It was discovered in the possession of the son of John Linnell, and first reprinted in the "Oxford" edition of Blake's works.

It is a poem almost unique among the poet's productions, and especially valuable to us, as it forms an intermediate stage, as it were, in the progress of his symbolism. In it we can see the actual movement of historical facts only half idealized into eternal symbols of the infinite. It is an idealized form of history, history raised and clarified into broader and more universal realms. Blake firmly believed that all natural events had spiritual causes, and, inversely, that human emotions and passions can and do send their waves vibrating through the infinite, producing there eternal flux and change. When he had given his defiance in a letter to Butts, "the sun stood trembling in heaven." "The bleat, the bark, bellow, and roar," he wrote in the "Auguries of Innocence," "Are waves that beat on Heaven's shore." This belief of his in the intercommunication of mortal and of spiritual essences spread itself to his study of history, and in the stirring events of the French Revolution he saw around him symbols of violent mental and spiritual development. Thus, in "The French Revolution," he kept the course of history before him, but it was history deprived of prosaic details and inherent with broader and higher significance. There is no trouble here in explaining the poetic atmosphere: there are no coined names whose meaning is to be found only after painful and laborious research. The drama is the drama of a nation's development, with Lafayette and the Abbé de Sieyès, representatives of the people, armed and rebellious, pitted against the Monarch, aided by his "ancientest Peer, Duke of Burgundy," Blake's description of whom has been already quoted.[31] Between them is Orleans, liberal but not revolutionary. The scene is the council-chamber, but the atmosphere is of immensity. The shadow or radiance that arises when these actors speak illuminates or saddens the whole universe. They are gods deliberating in fiery dispute on some Olympian mount. This treatment of history has immense possibilities, and, it must be confessed, Blake has made, in this mere fragment, excellent use of the facts given to him. That wonderful passage describing the Duke of Burgundy has a definite air of finality about it, nor does the voice of the Abbé de Sieyès fail to move our hearts:

THE SPEECH OF THE ABBÉ

> Hear, O heavens of France! the voice of the people, arising from valley and hill,
> O'erclouded with power. Hear the voice of the valleys, the voice of meek cities,
> Mourning oppressèd on village and field, till the village and field is a waste.
> For the husbandman weeps at blights of the fife, and blasting of trumpets consume
> The souls of mild France; the pale mother nourishes her child to the deadly slaughter.
> When the heavens were seel'd with a stone, and the terrible sun clos'd in an orb, and the moon
> Rent from the nations, and each star appointed for watchers of night,
> The millions of spirits immortal were bound in the ruins of sulphur heaven
> To wander enslav'd; black, depress'd in dark ignorance, kept in awe with the whip

---

[31] See page 60.

To worship terrors, bred from the blood of revenge and breath of desire
In bestial forms, or more terrible men; till the dawn of our peaceful morning,
Till dawn, till morning, till the breaking of clouds, and swelling of winds, and the universal voice;
Till man raise his darkened limbs out of the caves of night. His eyes and his heart
Expand—Where is Space? where, O Sun, is thy dwelling? where thy tent, O faint, slumb'rous Moon?
Then the valleys of France Shall cry to the soldier: "Throw down thy sword and musket,
And run and embrace the meek peasant." Her Nobles shall hear and shall weep, and put off
The red robe of terror, the crown of oppression, the shoes of contempt, and unbuckle
The girdle of war from the desolate earth. Then the Priest in his thund'rous cloud
Shall weep, bending to earth, embracing the valleys, and putting his hand to the plough,
Shall say: "No more I curse thee; but now will I bless thee: no more in deadly black
Devour thy labour; nor lift up a cloud in thy heavens, O laborious plough;
That the wild raging millions, that wander in forests, and howl in law-blasted wastes,
Strength madden'd with slavery, honesty bound in the dens of superstition,
May sing in the village, and shout in the harvest, and woo in pleasant gardens
Their once savage loves, now beaming with knowledge, with gentle awe adornèd;
And the saw, and the hammer, the chisel, the pencil, the pen, and the instruments

> Of heavenly song sound in the wilds once for-bidden, to teach the laborious ploughman
> And shepherd, deliver'd from clouds of war, from pestilence, from night-fear, from murder,
> From falling, from stifling, from hunger, from cold, from slander, discontent and sloth,
> That walk in beasts and birds of night, driven back by the sandy desert,
> Like pestilent fogs round cities of men; and the happy earth sing in its course,
> The mild peaceable nations be openèd to heaven, and men walk with their fathers in bliss."

The first book of this poem finishes abruptly, and in all probability we shall never see those remaining six books, completed, the advertisement to this volume tells us, but never published. There is, however, another fragment – "A Song of Liberty"—engraved about 1792 and affixed in one copy to the end of "The Marriage of Heaven and Hell"—which has the air of being, in tone at least, associated with the period that saw the production of "The French Revolution" and "America." This work, which is written in rhythmical prose, or free verse, is connected both with "Thel" and with "The French Revolution" in idea. It closes on the cry "Everything that lives is holy!" and recounts the progress of the revolutionary enthusiasm which seemed to a man like Blake to be transforming the world. England feels the tremor of new forces. America is arising to liberty. France is rending down its dungeons. Spain is bursting "the barriers of old Rome." Rome itself is casting its keys into the deep. Everything is breaking its frozen bonds and crying "Empire is no more, and now the Lion and the Wolf shall cease." With political restriction, too, religious restriction is being shattered, and youth and impulse are rising to their own once more.

With the "Visions of the Daughters of Albion," engraved in 1793, we are in a new realm of prophecy, derived but somehow different from the earlier works. In this year Blake removed his residence to 13 Hercules Buildings, Lambeth, the house probably that is now numbered 23 Hercules Road. He seems to have felt occasional fits of depression, for we find a note in one of his manuscript books – "I say I shan't live five years. And if I live one it will be a wonder." As we know, he was to live another thirty-four. He was still full of enthusiasm for the Revolution, however, and for another year or two he presented works whose main aim was to celebrate liberty–liberty, be it noted again, personal, social, and political. In these works the plea is threefold–against personal restriction, against restriction in matters of sex, and against tyrannous government.

There is a distinct 'plot' in "The Daughters of Albion," as there is in most of the early prophecies. Oothoon is a maiden, "the soft soul of America," who, loving and beloved by Theotormon, has been seized and violated by Bromion. Theotormon is jealous and binds them back to back with fetters of iron: but the daughters of Albion gather round her and sing their songs of more spiritual love, showing that mortal stain does not defile the pure innocence of the soul. The whole poem is an outburst against restrictive law and reason. Oothoon is at once the spirit of love who touches earth in her innocence, and is condemned therefor, and the spirit of poetry, bound in by shackling laws and commandments. The tragedy here is twofold, for in the jealousy that is born of law and reason Theotormon suffers as well as Oothoon. It is to be noted that Blake did not, as Mr Ellis declares, enunciate a doctrine of 'free love' promiscuously exercised: but rather sought to lay stress on the facts that mortal love did not stain the soul fabric, and that restrained desire was no less sinful than desires in their active form. In this he is the direct follower of Christ. He has nothing but condemnation for false modesty

THE CRY OF OOTHOON

"I cry: Love! Love! Love! happy, happy Love! free as the mountain wind!
Can that be love, that drinks another as a sponge drinks water,
That clouds with jealousy his nights, with weep-
ings all the day,
To spin a web of age around him, grey and hoary, dark:
Till his eyes sicken at the fruit that hangs before his sight?
Such is self-love that envies all, a creeping skeleton,
With lamplike eyes, watching around the frozen marriage
bed!"

"Does the sun walk, in glorious raiment, on the secret floor
Where the cold miser spreads his gold; or does the bright cloud
    drop
On his stone threshold? Does his eye behold the beam that
    brings
Expansion to the eye of pity? or will he bind himself
Beside the ox to thy hard furrow? Does not that mild beam
    blot
The bat, the owl, the glowing tiger, and the king of night?
The sea-fowl takes the wintry blast for a cov'ring to her limbs,
And the wild snake the pestilence to adorn him with gems and
    gold;
And trees, and birds, and beasts, and men behold their eternal
    joy.
Arise, you little glancing wings, and sing your infant joy!
Arise, and drink your bliss, for everything that lives is holy!"

In this poem, the "Visions of the Daughters of Albion," we are perplexed at times by references to America or "to the voice of slaves beneath the sun, and children bought with money"–half-symbolic, half-literal utterances that come from the lips of a mystic and social politician. In "America: A Prophecy," engraved in the same year, 1793, those symbolic references are seen rapidly passing into mental myth, just as Blake himself was moving swiftly from resentment at mortal wrongs to hatred of supernatural restraints. All through his life Blake showed a progress from perception of the phenomena of life to the perception of the mental and of the spiritual, and this development from the only half-symbolic figures of "The French Revolution" through the references to America in "The Daughters of Albion" onward to the prophecy of "America" itself, is in line with the rest of his mental advancement.

The whole of the 'plot' of "America" is symbolic, and, although Washington does appear as a visionary actor on its stage, he has not even such fleshly raiment as had the Abbé de Sieyès or the Duke of Burgundy. The idea that lies behind this poem connects it closely with "The Daughters of Albion," for it too has its praises of earthly passion, this time as keeping alive the desire for the infinite and for incorporeal liberty. America is here chosen as the seat of spiritual revolt, as much because it is the country of the West, the region of Tharmas, of earthly passion, as because Blake must have heard a great deal of its struggle for independence from the lips of his friend Tom Paine, who had himself been one of the chief figures in the war then over. The poem, as a poem, has not much value. There are lines or passages in it of wonderful excellence, as, for example, that "I know thee, I have found thee, and I will not let thee go," so reminiscent of a splendid lyric by Mr Bridges, or else that passage on page 5, wrought amid a bevy of frightful figures, describing the joy and incredulous wonder of a liberated people:

> "Let the slave grinding at the mill run out into the field,
> Let him look up into the heavens and laugh in the bright air:
> Let the enchainèd soul, shut up in darkness and in sighing,
> Whose face has never seen a smile in thirty weary years,
> Rise and look out: his chains are loose, his dungeon doors are open,
> And let his wife and children return from the oppressor's scourge.
> They look behind at every step, and believe it is a dream,
> Singing: "The sun has left his blackness, and has found a fresher morning,
> And the fair moon rejoices in the clear and cloudless night:
> For Empire is no more, and now the Lion and the
> Wolf shall cease."

Such an image of regenerated humanity, freed from its fetters, must be contrasted with the vision of "Europe: A Prophecy," engraved in 1794, and displaying in bitter wise the long sleep of Europe under the oppressive rule of those churches which had lost the secret and the message of Christ. It is a vision of what Blake most hated—hypocrisy, law, restraint, commandment. It is almost Shelley's vision of "Prometheus Unbound," with God the tyrannous ruler over everything, only differing from it in that Blake's God gains power not only through priestcraft, but through false science and erroneous philosophy as well. In both, however, mankind lies chained, as in that design of Europe where spiders' webs net in the words, and human figures lie clasped in the clinging veils of material phenomena, or of tyrannous political power, according to the way we read the poem. Like "Prometheus," "Europe" too ends in a prophecy of an awakening, when strife rises first in the fields of France, not merely social strife, but that mental warfare which is more deadly and more severe, because dealing with matters of the mind and not with evanescent, bodily things. Blake, mild as he was, remained a fighter to the end of his life, but his warfare was mostly concerned with the oppressive forces of the mind. He had as personal a hatred for Urizen, his personification of the tyrannous reason, as any slave could have for a brutal taskmaster. He abhorred the senseless war of nations when "the God of War is drunk with blood" and "Ghosts glut the throat of Hell," but he was ever ready to don his spiritual armour:

> Bring me my bow of burning gold!
>   Bring me my arrows of desire!
> Bring me my spear! O clouds, unfold!
>   Bring me my chariot of fire!
>
> I will not cease from mental fight,
>   Nor shall my sword sleep in my hand,
> Till we have built Jerusalem
>   In England's green and pleasant land.[32]

Blake spiritualized, almost out of ken, the forces of revolt.

It is possible that the excesses of the French Revolution gradually drew Blake away from an enthusiasm for the events on the Continent, but it is much more probable that the mystical turn of his mind was leading him beyond the symbolic presentation of history to a world having no limits of time or of place. In 1794 he produced "The (First) Book of Urizen," in 1795 "The Song of Los," The Book of Los," and "The Book of Ahania." All these are connected together as being shorter prophecies and as preparing the way for the longer prophecies of his last years.

"The (First) Book of Urizen"–there were no other books published–has for its plot the separation of Urizen from the Eternals. Its "Preludium" gives Blake's more mystic doctrine of poetic inspiration:

---

[32] Preface to "Milton." (see page 91)

> Eternals! I hear you call gladly.
> Dictate swift winged words, and fear not
> To unfold your dark visions of torment.

Later on he was to write to his friend Butts that he had written "Milton" "from immediate dictation" and therefore "can praise it, since I dare not pretend to be any other than the secretary." This, of course, did not prevent his putting on the title-pages of all his productions: "The Author and Printer William Blake."

"The Book of Urizen," as a whole, is a fine poem. The symbolism is a little difficult, but the story is a good one apart from its inner meaning. The "self-contemplating shadow" of Urizen breaks from eternity, and Los is set to watch his progress:

> For Eternals to confine
> The obscure separation alone.

In the light of eternal space, under the stars of the firmament, in lurid darkness, Los stands, binding with "rivets of iron and brass" Urizen's monstrous changes.

> Ages on ages roll'd over him;
> In stony sleep ages roll'd over him,
> Like a dark waste stretching, changeable,
> By earthquakes riv'n, belching sullen fires:
> On ages roll'd ages in ghastly
> Sick torment; around him in whirlwinds
> Of darkness the eternal Prophet howl'd,
> Beating still on his rivets of iron,
> Pouring solder of iron; dividing
> The horrible night into watches

until even, in this vast æon of eternal time, Los, spirit of prophecy, grows afraid, viewing the terrible changes which convulse Urizen's awful frame.

> All the myriads of Eternity,
> All the wisdom and the joy of life

> Roll like a sea around him:
> Except what his little orbs
> Of sight by degrees unfold,
> And now his eternal life,
> Like a dream, was obliterated.

And, seeing him thus, Los pities, and from his pity springs Enitharmon, his Emanation, the symbol of his softer qualities. But Enitharmon, the quiet spirit of loveliness, bears a man-child, and Los, who had first succoured it, feels the bonds of jealousy pressing on his breast. The child is named Orc, and Los, in his madness and fury, influenced by the frozen passions of Urizen, chains him to a rock "with the Chains of Jealousy." The net of Urizen has spread. His monstrous changes have swept over all, covering everything with the devastating nets of science and false religion. Only Puzon, spirit of revolt, calls a few brave comrades together and parts from the earth.

It is a drama whose scene is infinity, and whose actors are the giant forms of personified desires and passions of ideally human shape. It has, what the best poems of Blake's have, a plot, definite and definitely conceived. "Europe" is but a half-formed idea, imperfectly conceived. The felicity of phrase which was so noticeable in some of the earlier of Blake's songs, seems to have returned here with a new radiance. Lines of beauty meet our gaze:

> Voices of terror
> Are heard, like thunders of autumn,
> When the cloud blazes over the harvests;

or,

> For Eternity stood wide apart,
> As the stars are apart from the earth.

We are reft suddenly to a vision-world of boundless space and time where the smallest manifestations of earth are magnified a thousandfold into the "flames of eternal fury":

> Sund'ring, dark'ning, thund'ring,
> Rent away with a terrible crash,

> Eternity roll'd wide apart,
> Wide asunder rolling;
> Mountainous, all around,
> Departing, departing, departing,
> Leaving ruinous fragments of life,
> Hanging, frowning cliffs, and, all between,
> An Ocean of voidness unfathomable. ...

"The Book of Los" and "The Book of Ahania," both engraved in 1795, culminating in the beautiful lament of Ahania, bring this Lambeth period of Blake's career to a glorious conclusion. "The Book of Los" relates in different words much the same story as that told in "Urizen"—of Urizen's separation and binding, of his changes and final degradation—but this time told with Los as the principal agent in the historical progress of events, and with more visions of the "old time,"

> When Love and Joy were adoration,
> And none impure were deem'd,
> Not eyeless Covet,
> Nor thin-lipp'd Envy,
> Nor bristled Wrath,
> Nor curlèd Wantonness—

but when all those qualities, or vices as they are now called, in the free light of a primitive, imaginative age, had upon them the full value of great virtues—that is to say, when what has become wantonness in this wicked world of ours was holy love, when selfish wrath was righteous and flamelike fury of prophetically inspired power.

The poetry of "The Book of Ahania" is at once more profound and more gentle than that of Los. It carries on the hint left at the close of "The Book of Urizen" where Fuzon, alone, withstands the tyrant's power. It relates how Fuzon, the spirit of inspired revolt, the spirit of Jesus, "flam'd furious" against the aggressive power of his father and struck him so that his soul, Ahania, parted from him and "fell down, a faint Shadow, wand'ring in chaos." It relates how Urizen prepared a poisoned arrow and slew Fuzon and how a tree of mystery, the tree of Good and Evil, grew around the aged form of the father, until it wholly enveloped him. The close is beautiful, the lament of Ahania in magnificent cadences of sorrowing music, a fitting close to this period of Blake's poetic creation.

THE LAMENT OF AHANIA

The lamenting voice of Ahania,
Weeping upon the Void!
And round the Tree of Fuzon,
Distant in solitary night,
Her voice was heard, but no form
Had she; but her tears from clouds
Eternal fell round the Tree.

And the voice cried: "Ah, Urizen! Love!
Flower of morning! I weep on the verge
Of nonentity—how wide the Abyss
Between Ahania and thee!

I lie on the verge of the deep;
I see thy dark clouds ascend;
I see thy black forests and floods,
A horrible waste to my eyes!

Weeping I walk over rocks,
Over dens, and thro' valleys of death
Why didst thou despise Ahania,
To cast me from thy bright presence
Into the World of Loneness?

I cannot touch his hand,
Nor weep on his knees, nor hear
His voice and bow, nor see his eyes
And joy, nor hear his footsteps; and
My heart leap at the lovely sound!
I cannot kiss the place
Whereon his bright feet have trod;

But I wander on the rocks
With hard necessity.

Where is my golden palace?
Where my ivory bed?
Where the joy of my morning hour?
Where the Sons of Eternity singing,

To awake bright Urizen, my King,
To arise to the mountain sport,
To the bliss of eternal valleys;

To awake my King in the morn,
To embrace Ahania's joy
On the breath of his open bosom,
From my soft cloud of dew to fall
In showers of life on his harvests?

. . . .

But now alone! over rocks, mountains,
Cast out from thy lovely bosom!
Cruel Jealousy, Selfish Fear,
Self-destroying! how can delight
Renew in these chains of darkness,
Where bones of beasts are strown
On the bleak and snowy mountains,
Where bones from the birth are buried
Before they see the light?

VI

WITH "Ahania" closes this period of Blake's shorter prophecies, the period he spent at Lambeth just before his departure for Felpham under the patronage of Hayley. "Vala," it is true, was written between 1796 and 1798, only a year or two after "Ahania," but not only does it differ largely from the shorter prophecies, but it was revised about 1802, its title changed from "Vala, or The Death and Judgement of the Ancient Man: A Dream of Nine Nights," to "The Four Zoas: The Torments of Love and Jealousy of Albion the Ancient Man," and great parts of it reworked and rewritten. It is the poem that connects for us the earlier works with the final "Milton" and "Jerusalem."

Just about the years 1795 and 1796 Blake was feeling more and more the pinch of poverty. His prophecies no one understood, and the sale for them cannot have been excessive. Most of his time must have been occupied in writing and in printing them, and, possibly because of their strange form and content, even the demand for ordinary engravings from him was lessening. In 1796, however, he seems to have made a determined effort to find some work or other of a remunerative character. In that year he produced three illustrations for an English translation of Bürger's romantic ballad of "Lenore," and was commissioned by the publisher Edwards to collaborate in a sumptuous volume of Young's "Night Thoughts." The designs for this work, evidently, were not considered very satisfactory. Only one part was published, the remainder being issued in 1802 illustrated by Stothard. Apparently little could be hoped for from this direction. Blake, however, when we take into consideration his temperament and his mystical aims, was not unfortunate in his patrons, and in the year 1797 a new man, Thomas Butts, came on the scene with an offer of a guinea each for fifty coloured drawings. Butts was not a mystic, nor was he an artist, but he seems to have taken a real liking for the poet, who was now just forty years of age, and he appears to have put no restraint on him either as regards choice of subject-matter for the designs or their treatment. For three years, then, Blake worked in this way, with the hounds of starvation ever at his door, part of his revolutionary enthusiasm gone, his poetic works despised, wondering perhaps where next he was to turn. In 1800 he was to be set at rest for a time at least, for in that year Flaxman introduced him to Hayley, a wealthy poetaster, and in September he set off for Felpham to be near his patron. Before we come to that Felpham visit, however, and the last two poems of Blake's writing, we may pause to glance at "Vala."

In 1797, as we have seen, this poem was written (it was never engraved), in a neat cursive hand, on scraps of paper which were often mere fragments of proof engravings. It was pencilled all through with illustrations. In later days, when writing "Milton" and "Jerusalem," Blake plagiarized himself, for huge passages of "Vala" he reproduced in these later works, apparently having given up the idea of presenting "Vala" to the world. Yet "Vala," taken as a whole, is by far the best of his last three productions. It has more sequence than "Jerusalem," more poetic beauty than "Milton." It presents itself to us as an epic of boundless infinitude, an epic beside which "Urizen" seems but a passionate and lyric outburst, an epic, not bound together closely in its development, perchance, but revealing beauties which constantly challenge our attention. The whole poem gleams with excellency of phrase and with melody of rhythmic musical form.

> O, I am weary! Lay thine hand upon me, or I faint,
> I faint beneath these beams of thine.
>
> . . . .
>
> Now I am nothing, and I sink,
> And on the bed of silence sleep, till thou wakest me.

Such a verse, sung by Enitharmon over Los, might have taken mortal shape from Shelley's spirit lips.

"Vala," too, is full of 'personal' utterance, cries and rejoicings which seem to come straight from the heart-depths of the poet. One such is that in the second Night, where Enion wails forth a cry that seems Blake's own:

THE PRICE OF EXPERIENCE

What is the price of Experience? Do men buy it for a song,
Or Wisdom for a dance in the street? No: it is bought with the price
Of all that a man hath—his house, his wife, his children.
Wisdom is sold in the desolate market where none come to buy,
And in the wither'd field where the farmer ploughs for bread in vain.

It is an easy thing to triumph in the summer's sun,
And in the vintage, and to sing on the waggon loaded with corn:
It is an easy thing to talk of patience to the afflicted,
To speak the laws of prudence to the houseless wanderer,
To listen to the hungry raven's cry in wintry season,
When the red blood is fill'd with wine and with the marrow of lambs.

It is an easy thing to laugh at wrathful elements:
To hear the dog howl at the wintry door, the ox in the slaughter-house moan;
To see a God on every wind and a blessing on every blast;
To hear sounds of Love in the thunderstorm that destroys our enemy's house;
To rejoice in the blight that covers his field, and the sickness that cuts off his children,
While our olive and vine sing and laugh round our door, and our children bring fruits and flowers.

Then the groan and the dolour are quite forgotten, and the slave grinding at the mill,
And the captive in chains, and the poor in the prison, and the soldier in the field

> When the shatter'd bone hath laid him groaning among the
>   happier dead:
> It is an easy thing to rejoice in the tents of prosperity–
> Thus would I sing and thus rejoice; but it is not so with me.

No, it was not so with Blake. He was tormented with the spectre of poverty on earth, with the Spectre of Reason and Restriction in the mental realms of his own devising.

In "Vala" there are songs of innocence beside melodies of despair, and the greater part of them of a surpassing beauty. The Shadow of Enitharmon goes forth and returns:

>   Now she was pale as snow,
> When the mountains and hills are cover'd over, and the
>   paths of men shut up;
> But, when her spirit return'd, as ruddy as a morning when
> The ripe fruit blushes into joy in Heaven's eternal halls.

Such lovely visions as these cheer us on our way through the dark mass of Blake's mystic thought. Nor does that thought here oppress us as it sometimes does in the two later prophecies. There are more passages here of what we might call ordinary poetry, unmingled with strange symbolic names and abstruse ideas. Such an one is the fine passage which Dr Sampson has well called "the Song of the Sinless Soul":

THE SONG OF THE SINLESS SOUL

> "Whose voice is this in the voice of the nourishing air,
> In the spirit of the morning, awaking the Soul from its grassy
>   bed?
> Where dost thou dwell? for it is thee I seek, and but for thee
> I must have slept eternally, nor have felt the dew of thy
>   morning.
> Look how the opening dawn advances with vocal harmony!
> Look how the beams foreshow the rising of some glorious
>   power!

The Sun is thine; he goeth forth in his majestic brightness.
O thou creating voice that callest and who shall answer thee?"

"Where dost thou flee, O Fair One! where dost thou seek thy
    happy place?
To yonder brightness? There I haste, for sure I came from
    thence,
Or I must have slept eternally, nor have felt the dew of
    morning."
"Eternally thou must have slept, nor have felt the morning
    dew,
But for yon nourishing Sun; 'tis that by which thou art risen.
The birds adore the Sun; the beasts rise up and play in his
    beams,
And every flower and every leaf rejoices in his light.
Then, O thou Fair One, sit thee down, for thou art as the
    grass,
Thou risest in the dew of morning, and at night art folded
    up."
"Alas! am I but a flower? Then will I sit me down;
Then will I weep; then I'll complain, and sigh for immortality,
And chide my maker, thee O Sun, that raisedst me to fall."
So saying she sat down and wept beneath the apple-trees.
"O! be thou blotted out, thou Sun, that raisedst me to trouble,
Thou gavest me a heart to crave, and raisedst me, thy
    phantom,
To feel thy heart, and see thy light, and wander here alone,
Hopeless, if I am like the grass, and so shall pass away."
"Rise, sluggish Soul! Why sitt'st thou here? why dost thou sit
    and weep?
Yon Sun shall wax old and decay, but thou shalt ever flourish.
The fruit shall ripen and fall down, and the flowers consume
    away,
But thou shalt still survive. Arise! O dry thy dewy tears!"
"Ha! shall I still survive? Whence came that sweet comforting
    voice?

And whence that voice of sorrow? O Sun! thou art nothing now to me:
Go on thy course rejoicing, and let us both rejoice together!
I walk among His flocks and hear the bleating of His lambs.
O! that I could behold His face and follow His pure feet!
I walk by the footsteps of His flocks. Come hither, tender flocks!
Can you converse with a pure Soul that seeketh for her Maker?
You answer not: then am I set your mistress in this garden.
I'll watch you and attend your footsteps. You are not like the birds
That sing and fly in the bright air; but you do lick my feet,
And let me touch your woolly backs: follow me as I sing;
For in my bosom a new Song arises to my Lord:
Rise up, O Sun! most glorious minister and light of day!
Flow on, ye gentle airs, and bear the voice of my rejoicing!
Wave freshly, clear waters, flowing around the tender grass;
And thou, sweet-smelling ground, put forth thy life in fruit and flowers!
Follow me, O my flocks, and hear me sing my rapturous song!
I will cause my voice to be heard on the clouds that glitter in the sun.
I will call, and who shall answer me? I shall sing; who shall reply?
For, from my pleasant hills, behold the living, living springs,
Running among my green pastures, delighting among my trees!
I am not here alone: my flocks, you are my brethren;
And you birds, that sing and adorn the sky, you are my sisters.
I sing, and you reply to my song; I rejoice, and you are glad.
Follow me, O my flocks! we will now descend into the valley.
O, how delicious are the grapes, flourishing in the sun!
How clear the spring of the rock, running among the golden sand!

> How cool the breezes of the valley! And the arms of the
>   branching trees
> Cover us from the sun: come and let us sit in the shade.
> My Luvah here hath plac'd me in a sweet and pleasant land,
> And given me fruits and pleasant waters, and warm hills and
>   cool valleys.
> Here will I build myself a house, and here I'll call on His name;
> Here I'll return, when I am weary, and take my pleasant rest."

Such a vision must have seemed a very delightful one to poor Blake, but it was one that was never to materialize for him in his lifetime. What did promise to develop into such an Earthly Paradise turned out to be almost a Hell of torment. He came to Felpham with the full hopes of one entering on a new life: he left it with bitterness and hate in his heart.

To understand this visit aright we must strive to keep clearly in our mind the trustful, proud, independent soul of Blake, and at the same time the character of this rich poetaster Hayley. Hayley was a well-educated man, intensely conceited, infinitely eager to be regarded as a patron of the arts. He had already won a name for his "Triumphs of Temper," a pitiful, sentimental production of no poetic worth, and was meditating lives of Cowper and of Romney. Blake, however, was ill-calculated to estimate his true nature, and in the year 1800 he must have come like a godsend. On August 26, 1799, the poet was writing to Cumberland: "As to myself, ... I live by miracle. I am painting small pictures from the Bible. For as to my engraving, in which art I cannot reproach myself with any neglect, I am laid by in a corner as if I did not exist, and since my Young's "Night Thoughts" have been published, even Johnson and Fuseli have discarded my graver. But as I know that he who works and has his health cannot starve, I laugh at fortune, and go on and on." In spite of his optimistic note, despair must often have entered into his heart. Flaxman, no doubt noticing his precarious state, evidently thought that Hayley would be the very man to help him, and on May 6, 1800, we find Blake writing to Hayley to condole with him on the death of an illegitimate son. That letter contains an unforgettable phrase: "The ruins of Time build mansions in Eternity"—a phrase in itself that might well have fired the curiosity of the patron. On September 12 it has been arranged that they are to set off to join Hayley at Felpham, and Blake in his enthusiasm writes a poetical letter to Flaxman in which he places him as his true guide in the heavens, beside Milton, Isaiah, Shakespeare, Paracelsus, and Behmen. On the 21st he is already in his new home, a cottage near Hayley's villa, and he is writing to express his delight to the "dear sculptor of Eternity," John Flaxman. He seems to have a renewed lease of life. "Mr Hayley received us with his usual brotherly affection. I have begun to work. Felpham is a sweet place for study, because it is more spiritual than London. Heaven opens here on all sides her golden gates; her windows are not obscured by vapours; voices of celestial inhabitants are most distinctly heard, and their forms more distinctly seen; and my cottage is also a shadow of their houses. ... Now begins a new life, because another covering of earth is shaken off." Everything he sees seems to be a premonition of future happiness. "I met a plough," he writes to Butts on the 23rd, "on my first going out at my gate the first morning after my arrival, and the ploughboy said to the ploughman, 'Father, the gate is open.'" In October we find him writing those verses to Butts about 'double vision' which I have already quoted. Hayley is decorating his villa with new designs, and commissions Blake to draw heads of Homer, Camoens, Ercilla, Ariosto, and Spenser for his study. The poet-artist is also entrusted with illustrations for some of Hayley's ballads. Everything seems to promise well.

When and how the clouds began to gather we cannot tell with accuracy, but we can re-form for ourselves a picture of those three years. Hayley was kind, but he wanted to lead Blake away from his visions. He tried to teach him Greek, and to admire Greek art. He read Klopstock to him. He attempted to induce him to take up miniature-painting in order to provide himself with a livelihood. Outwardly Blake had to seem grateful, but inwardly he fumed. The very kindness of Hayley made the matter worse. Happily for the poet, however, he had a note book, and in that he penned down in satirical verses his opinion of his patron, and prevented his rage becoming too evident on the surface.

> Thy friendship oft has made my heart to ache,

he writes on one occasion,

> Do be my enemy—for friendship's sake.

He is quite clearly exasperated. He cannot be rude, for no rudeness has been offered to him. At the same time he feels his very being is slowly becoming crushed and fettered. He abhors miniature-painting:

> When H(ayle)y finds out what you cannot do,
> That is the very thing he'll set you to;
> If you break not your neck, 'tis not his fault,
> But pecks of poison are not peeks of salt.

Again:

> I write the rascal thanks, till he and I
> With thanks and compliments are quite drawn dry.

Reading these epigrams, it must seem quite obvious that such a position could not last for long. Indeed, it is a wonder that Blake did not leave Felpham long before he did. As it was, he apparently did not finally make up his mind until April 1803, and was not back in London until September, when he settled down in rooms at 17 South Molton Street. Before he left Felpham, however, another vexatious incident had occurred to trouble his mind for a few months. Coming into his cottage garden one day in August, he found there a stranger named Skofield, a private in the 1st Royal Dragoons, and requested him to leave. The man had, without Blake's knowledge, been invited by the gardener to assist in the garden, and returned him an impertinent answer. An altercation ensued, only to end when Blake, taking the man by the elbows, ran him down the road for about fifty yards. The result was that the soldier made a complaint against the poet, averring that he had uttered seditious sentiments against the King. Blake easily provided bail, and was acquitted at the Chichester sessions, but not without mental torment to himself. It was after this that the name Skofield became affixed to one of his worst symbolic figures of iniquity. Everything seemed to have gone wrong at once. He felt himself on all sides misunderstood, a genius fettered by circumstance, a poet of visions doomed to find his visions mocked at and himself despised.

TO THOMAS BUTTS

O! why was I born with a different face?
Why was I not born like the rest of my race?
When I look, each one starts; when I speak, I offend;
Then I'm silent and passive, and lose every friend.

Then my verse I dishonour, my pictures despise,
My person degrade, and my temper chastise;
And the pen is my terror, my pencil my shame;
All my talents I bury, and dead is my fame.

I am either too low, or too highly priz'd;
When elate I'm envied; when meek I'm despis'd.[33]

It was in the midst of this trouble and misery of three years that Blake wrote the major part of "Milton" and "Jerusalem," works which he began to engrave soon after his return to town. "Milton" was finished in 1808, "Jerusalem" not until 1820.

Milton is obviously an *apologia pro pensis suis*. Milton is Blake, just as he is Los, the spirit of prophetic power and inspiration, hindered on all sides by the dulling facts and torments of existence. Personal resentment mingles in it with the roar and the turmoil of the furnaces of Los. Blake, however, never worked well when in a mortal temper with some material hindrance or corporeal enemy. He needed his hindrances and his enemies to be mental before they adduced fine poetry from him. Hatred made his mind too chaotic, his poetry too bitterly fragmentary ever to produce such marvels of music and of emotion as are to be found, for example, in "Vala." "Milton," therefore, beyond a few passages, is rather a dull affair. It begins, certainly, with what is one of Blake's finest lyrics, but the tone is not preserved through the entirety of the poem.

---

[33] From a letter to Thomas Butts, dated August 16, 1803.

PREFACE TO "MILTON"

  And did those feet in ancient time
    Walk upon England's mountain green?
  And was the holy Lamb of God
    On England's pleasant pastures seen?

  And did the Countenance Divine
    Shine forth upon our clouded hills?
  And was Jerusalem builded here
    Among these dark Satanic Mills?

  Bring me my bow of burning gold!
    Bring me my arrows of desire!
  Bring me my spear! O clouds, unfold!
    Bring me my chariot of fire!

  I will not cease from mental fight,
    Nor shall my sword sleep in my hand,
  Till we have built Jerusalem
    In England's green and pleasant land.

  This is of Blake's finest utterance, full of inspiration, and inwrought with eternal beauty. The question of *its* loveliness can never be debated, but we may cast a doubt concerning those forty and odd pages that follow, full of symbolic and only half-understandable poetry. The passages of glowing words are rarer than in "Vala." We may still have visions of beauty as of that "pleasant shadow" on page 31 where

             All the weak and weary
  Like Women and Children were taken away as on wings
  Of dovelike softness, and shadowy habitations prepared for
    them,

and where

  Thou hearest the nightingale begin the Song of Spring:
  The lark, sitting upon his earthy bed, just as the morn

> Appears, listens silent; then, springing from the waving cornfield, loud
> He leads the Choir of Day—trill! trill! trill! trill!
> Mounting upon the wings of light into the great
> Expanse,
> Re-echoing against the lovely blue and shining heavenly Shell;
> His little throat labours with inspiration; every feather
> On throat and breast and wings vibrates with the effluence divine.
> All Nature listens silent to him, and the awful Sun
> Stands still upon the mountain looking on this little Bird
> With eyes of soft humility and wonder, love, and awe.
> Then loud from their green covert all the Birds begin their song;
> The Thrush, the Linnet and the Goldfinch, Robin, and Wren
> Awake the Sun from his sweet reverie upon the mountain:
> The Nightingale again essays his song, and thro' the day
> And thro' the night warbles luxuriant; every
> Bird of song
> Attending his loud harmony with admiration and love.
> This is a Vision of the lamentation of Beulah over Ololon.

But such passages seem scarcer than in those other books, more detached from the main thread of the poetic narrative.

The truth is that in this poem, and in "Jerusalem, the Emanation of the Giant Albion," the separate plates forming the pages of the work seem almost interchangeable. Dozens of pages lack connexion either with what precedes or with what comes after. Many must have been hastily introduced between the year in which the engraving was started, 1804, and the year it was completed, 1820. "Jerusalem," however, more than "Milton," bears to us the true beauty of poetry. Most of it must have been written when Blake's anger against Hayley had died down, as we know it did die down about the year 1805. After he had left the clutches of the patron he was able to look back upon him with kindly feelings. On the other hand, "Jerusalem" has no 'plot.' Liberty, certainly, is the main theme, but we lose sight of it in many separate passages. The introduction to the poem informs us that it will relate

> Of the sleep of Ulro! And of the passage through
> Eternal Death! And of the awaking to Eternal Life!

but little is to be seen in the work as a whole. There is a seeming scheme in the four chapters, addressed to the Public, to the Jews, to the Deists, and to the Christians respectively—but the introductions to those chapters have nothing to do with the separate contents. Possibly they were interpolated long after the main part of the poem was penned. There are pages, too, in "Jerusalem," not only of detached phrasing, but of hopeless triviality and meaningless enumeration. Let anyone open his "Jerusalem" at page 16 and read there:

> And the Forty Counties of England are thus divided in the
> 	Gates
> Of Reuben, Norfolk, Suffolk, Essex; Simeon,
> Lincoln, York, Lancashire;
> Levi, Middlesex, Kent, Surrey; Judah, Somerset,
> Glouster, Wiltshire;
> Dan, Cornwall ...

and so on, until the entire series is exhausted. There is no poetry in that, nor is there philosophy. Messrs Ellis and Yeats describe this passage as belonging to "a set of anatomical as well as psychological correspondences forming a secret language, an arcanum, to which Blake has not left a complete key," and his failure to leave that key does not seem to matter much. Yet fine poetry exists in "Jerusalem" too, and it only seems a pity that it should be rendered so inaccessible by the dreary symbolism with which it is surrounded.

> And thus the Spectre spake: Wilt thou go on to destruction
> Till thy life is all taken away by this deceitful friendship?
> He drinks thee up like water: like wine he pours thee
> Into his tuns: thy Daughters are trodden in his vintage:
> He makes thy Sons the trampling of his bulls, they are plow'd
> And harrow'd for his profit, lo! thy stolen
> 	Emanation
> Is his Garden of Pleasure! All the Spectres of his Sons mock
> 	thee.

> Look how they scorn thy once admired palaces, now in ruins
> Because of Albion, because of deceit and friendship. ...

So we read on page 7, and, viewing there behind the personal resentment at Hayley's friendship touches of poetic utterance, we are tempted to read further, but what do we find?

>   Lo!
> Hand has peopled Babel and Nineveh; Hyle, Ashur and
>   Aram;
> Coban's son is Nimrod: his son Cush is adjoin'd to Aram,
> By the daughter of Babel. ...
> Kox is the father of Shem and Ham and Japheth ...

—meaningless words repeated and reiterated for several lines, leading on again, after a dreary desert, to another passage of loveliness. What are we to make of this? It draws us naturally to a consideration of the question often put forward—was Blake improving as he advanced? Are these three longer prophecies his master pieces?

Personally, I do not think that anyone who has not been led astray by Blake's symbolic message would dare to suggest that the later poems were superior as poems to the "Songs of Innocence and of Experience." These longer prophecies are entire failures when considered as a whole. In his last idea of producing "epics as long as Homer" and "tragedies as long as Macbeth," Blake was working out his own destruction. He was entirely and wholly a lyrist. Even the passages in those longer books which are memorable are the short utterances of immediate passion. A poem able to be written at a single sitting—it might be of hours—was the limit of his art. The lyrics, of course, were all of this sudden type, and even the best of the shorter prophecies, I feel, must have been written practically from a moment's mood. Already I have noted Blake's lack of plot-weaving power, his 'plot' in all the lyrics and shorter prophecies being but an emotion vividly portrayed in many different guises. We may, certainly, have a series of such emotions, or emotions of contrasting form, but never a definite story woven out of them. Each emotion is distinct—as distinct as he believed colours and ideas ought to be upon the painter's canvas. I have often wondered whether Blake might have given us something stupendous in his poetry, as he has in his art of design in the "Job" series, if he had been willing to adopt the plot of some other writer. What he might have achieved had he been like Shakespeare and utilized the vague ideas and half-formed conceptions of his predecessors can only be hazily conjectured.

But such speculations are futile, for Blake, without his visions and his independence, would not have been Blake. It is momentary vision that transforms all his pictures and his poems—that double vision which changes earthly things into eternal symbols, which pierces below the material into the spiritual, which, conversely, turns abstract emotions into human form, gives to Pity a name and to Love a human habitation and a resting-place. What, after all, we have to remember is that Blake, as a poet, must be studied emotionally for the pure beauty of his verse and for such symbolic message as he is able to give to us without having recourse to huge depressing tabulæ of well-nigh meaningless names. Mr Ellis means it as a compliment, but it is truly a condemnation of "Jerusalem," when he says that any adequate commentary on that poem would be ten times as long as the poem itself. If we have such lengthy commentaries, then vision and poetry cease to be vision and poetry and come to be cryptic philosophy.

In poetry, when he was not misled by this philosophy, his aim was the final and only true one. In his "Public Address," written probably about 1810, he declares that he has heard people say, "'Give me the ideas: it does not matter what words you put them into,' and others say, 'Give me the design: it is no matter for the execution.' These people knew enough of artifice but little enough of art. Ideas cannot be given but in their minutely appropriate words. Nor can a design be made without its minutely appropriate execution." The man who first realized this inevitable communion between content and form achieved his end in the finer among the lyrics and in the best of the shorter prophecies. It is false adoration of Blake for his admirers, often from a mere spirit of obstinacy, to profess poetic enthusiasm for the longer works, which are merely, with the exception of scattered passages, a chaos of heterogeneous pages. Blake was undoubtedly "the greatest of English Mystics," but I doubt whether "adequate study and appreciation" of his more concealed mysticism will raise the fame that is his unquestioned from the songs and from the other lyrics, from the flaming terrors of Urizen, the lamentation of Ahania, the gentle voice of Thel murmuring those exquisite premonitions of eternity from distant and peaceful vales of dreamlike innocence. As in the case of Shakespeare, we must strive to keep "this side idolatry" and restrain too keen enthusiasts from reaving Blake away from poetry into dryer realms of mystic, even if often sublime, philosophy.

VII

THE story of Blake's life after the production of "Jerusalem" concerns rather the world of art than the world of poetry. We hear about 1809 a vague reference to "Barry: A Poem" and a "Book of Moonlight," but these, if ever written, are now non-extant. On the other hand, the best known of Blake's designs belong to the years 1805 to 1827. He died in the very act of putting finishing touches to his illustrations for "La Divina Commedia." The famous "Grave" designs were finished by 1805 and issued in 1808 as engraved by Schiavonetti. Originally these had been commissioned by Cromek on the understanding that Blake should be employed to do the engraving. Cromek, however, an astute rascal, soon repudiated the agreement, paid Blake twenty guineas for twelve designs, and reaped a horrid glory from this robbing of the poet. The blow must have been a severe one to Blake, who then, as at other times, was desperately in need of money. "A petty sneaking knave I knew," he writes in his note-book. "O! Mr Gromek, how do ye do?" and:

> Cromek loves artists as he loves his meat;
> He loves the Art; but 'tis the art to cheat.

Not always, however, was he able to relieve himself thus in satire, and there is a pitiful note in the Rossetti manuscript: "Tuesday, Jany. 20, 1807, between Two and seven in the Evening, Despair." During the next few years little work would seem to have come his way. Butts certainly remained a faithful friend, and the Countess of Egremont purchased a painting, "The Last Judgment," in 1808, but such is not enough to keep even the flesh and bone of an artist together. Blake still worked on, however, and in 1809 opened an exhibition of pictures at 28 Broad Street. This probably was not a success from the monetary point of view, but it allowed him in his catalogue to vent his feelings in regard to false and to true art. During the run of the exhibition he also issued a prospectus for an engraving to illustrate "The Canterbury Pilgrims." This engraving he issued on October 8, 1810. About the same time he was writing in the Rossetti manuscript the set of controversial verses known as "The Everlasting Gospel." Enough has been said about Blake's idea of Christ to make it plain that this portrait of Jesus was the direct antithesis of the portrait painted by the Churches. For Blake Christ was not mild, or humble, or over pure. He was a flaming artist-soul, working by impulse.

THE PRIDE OF CHRIST

God wants not man to humble himself:
That is the trick of the Ancient Elf.
This is the race that Jesus ran:
Humble to God, haughty to man,
Cursing the Rulers before the people
Even to the Temple's highest steeple,
And when He humbled Himself to God
Then descended the cruel rod.
"If Thou humblest Thyself, Thou humblest Me,
Thou also dwell'st in Eternity.
Thou art a Man: God is no more:
Thy own Humanity learn to adore,
For that is My Spirit of life.
Awake, arise to spiritual strife,
And Thy revenge abroad display
In terrors at the last Judgement Day."
Can that which was of woman born,
In the absence of the morn,
When the Soul fell into sleep,
And Archangels round it weep,
Shooting out against the light
Fibres of a deadly night,
Reason(ing) upon its own dark fiction,
In doubt which is self-contradiction?
Humility is only doubt,
And does the sun and moon blot out,

> Rooting over with thorns and stems
> The buried soul and all its gems.
> This life's five windows of the soul
> Distorts the Heavens from pole to pole,
> And leads you to believe a lie
> When you see with, not thro', the eye
> That was born in a night, to perish in a night,
> When the soul slept in the beams of light.[34]

These verses are interesting for a student of Blake's ideas, but they never reach even the hem of the robe of poetry. Between 1811 and 1817 Blake disappears entirely from our ken. What he did for a living during those terrible weary winters of want and obscurity we can only guess. We have none of his letters for this period, and but one or two engravings. In 1818, however, we know that he was introduced to John Linnell, one of the chief benefactors of his later years, and in 1819 was introduced by Linnell to Varley, the phrenologist. For the latter he executed a series of "Visionary Heads," including the famous "Ghost of a Flea," and for Linnell he produced a mass of work that ended only with the Dante designs of 1826-27. In 1820, the year when he completed the engraving of "Jerusalem," he started his most famous painting of "The Last Judgment" and worked at a set of delicious little woodcuts for Thornton's "Pastorals of Virgil." The year following he removed to what was to be his home for the rest of his life, 3 Fountain Court, Strand. The water-colours in illustration of the "Book of Job" were started there in 1821, to the order of Butts, and completed in 1825. In the latter year he started his Dante drawings for Linnell, and these he continued to the very day of his death. In the autumn of August 1826 he felt symptoms of sickness, sickness that seemed to come in waves of recurring fury. His last extant letter, that sent on July 3, 1827, to John Linnell, tells its own tale. "I find I am not so well as I thought," he writes. "I must not go on in a youthful style. However, I am upon the mending hand to-day." A month later the symptoms of fatal disease were more pronounced than ever. The story of his last day may be told

---

[34] Blake is here trying to distinguish between sensuous and spiritual vision. The one "sees through the eye" and is false; the other bathes in the radiance of eternity.

in the words of his earliest biographer, John Tatham, whom he met two years before his death.

"Life," says Tatham, "like a dying flame, flashed once more, gave one more burst of animation, during which he was cheerful, and free from the tortures of his approaching end; he thought he was better, and, as he was sure to do, asked to look at the work over which he was occupied when seized with his last attack. It was a coloured print of the Ancient of Days striking the first circle of the Earth, done expressly by commission for the writer of this. After he had worked upon it he exclaimed: 'There, I have done all I can! I hope Mr Tatham will like it.' He threw it suddenly down and said: 'Kate, you have been a good wife; I will draw your portrait.' She sat near his bed, and he made a drawing which, though not a likeness, is finely touched and expressed. He then threw that down, after having drawn for an hour, and began to sing Hallelujahs and songs of joy and triumph which Mrs Blake described as being truly sublime in music and in verse; he sang loudly and with true ecstatic energy, and seemed so happy that he had finished his course, that he had run his race, and that he was shortly to arrive at the goal, to receive the prize of his high and eternal calling. After having answered a few questions concerning his wife's means of living after his decease ... his spirit departed like the sighing of a gentle breeze, and he slept in company with the mighty ancestors he had formerly depicted. He passed from death to an immortal life on the 12th of August, 1827, being in his sixty-ninth year. Such was the entertainment of the last hour of his life. His bursts of gladness made the room peal again. The walls rang and resounded with the beatific symphony. It was a prelude to the hymns of the saints. It was an overture to the choir of heaven. It was a response of the angels."

BIBLIOGRAPHY

The following list contains the titles of some books which may be specially recommended for the further study of Blake and his work.

TEXT

"The Poetical Works of William Blake," edited by John Sampson. Oxford University Press. This does not contain the full text of the three longer Prophecies, but is the standard text for all the other poems.

"The Poetical Works of William Blake," edited and annotated by Edwin J. Ellis. Chatto and Windus. 2 vols.

"The Works of William Blake, Poetic, Symbolic, and Critical," edited by E. J. Ellis and W. B. Yeats. Bernard Quaritch. 3 vols. The prophetic books are here reproduced in lithograph, and there is a lengthy commentary, often rather difficult to follow, on the mystical ideas of Blake.

"Milton" and "Jerusalem" have been issued by E. R. D. Maclagan and A. G. B. Russell in 2 vols., and should be read in this edition.

BIOGRAPHY AND CRITICISM

A. Gilchrist: "The Life of William Blake." 1863 and 1880. Reprinted 1907. This is the standard Life, and contains reproductions taken from Blake's own copper plates.

A. C. Swinburne: "William Blake: A Critical Essay." 1868 and 1906. An enthusiastic defence of Blake and his poetry.

R. Garnett: "William Blake: Painter and Poet." 1895.

E. J. Ellis: "The Real Blake: A Portrait Biography." 1907. An attempt to present a portrait of Blake the man.

A. Symons: "William Blake." 1907. One of the most interesting general essays on the poet.

P. Berger: "William Blake, Poet and Mystic." English translation, 1914. A careful and painstaking study of Blake's poetic methods and symbolic aims. This has become a standard critical study.

E. de Selincourt: "William Blake." 1909.

G. K. Chesterton: "William Blake." 1910.

C. Gardner: "William Blake the Man." 1919.

Particularly useful will be found "The Letters of William Blake; together with a Life by Frederic Tatham," ed. A. G. B. Russell. (Methuen.) Some attention should also be paid to Blake's pictorial art. Most of the principal designs have been reproduced in one or other of the critical volumes given above. The British Museum have published a set of twelve postcards giving reproductions of plates in their possession.

www.ingramcontent.com/pod-product-compliance
Lightning Source LLC
Chambersburg PA
CBHW020428010526
44118CB00010B/480